Becoming the Superman

Everything you need to succeed

Anthony Reif

ISBN: 0-9966751-0-8
ISBN-13: 978-0-9966751-0-9
(Living Beyond Life, LLC)

Dedication

There is only one person who I could ever think of dedicating this book to. She has done more for me than anyone else I know and continues to be an integral part of my life and the completion of this book. This book is dedicated to my dear mother and editor, Karen.

Acknowledgements

It has been a long journey for me to learn what it means to be the superman and there are a lot of people that have helped me along the way. I have to first thank my editor, Karen, for reading my rough drafts and giving me advice along the way. Without her dedication, this book never would have been published. I have to thank my friends who have influenced sections of the book whether they know it or not. They were there along the way to inspire, support, and encourage me to keep going. I would like to thank everyone who has helped free me from believing I was just an ordinary human being, as I hope to do for each and every one of you. Of course, I have to thank my parents as well and my brothers for teaching me how to be the person I am today. Without everything and everyone that has been there along the path of my life, I would be in a completely different place and probably not as happy. Everyone else in my life, whether they know it or not, has had an impact on this book as well and I hope they know how grateful I am to have had them in my life.

Author's Note

If you knew what I know, you could do and have everything you want. The only thing stopping you is the belief that you cannot. Everything we believe is real, has created our world and limits us. Choose instead to think and feel the way you want to be instead of the way you are. The path of the superman is one without limit. It allows people to be their ideal self instead of being stuck in what they are. This lifestyle creates an ideal world for you and others.

A superman is not necessarily a man. In this book, I refer to human beings as a whole, male and female, not meaning a specific gender. Please understand this to open yourself to progress and willingness to improve. There has been a lot of politically correct ideology flooding the world these days, as it does with the development of a civilized society. In my book I made the choice to use the male term: superman and supermen. If you've read the book, you already know I encourage everybody to learn and teach the message and lifestyle of the supermen to all other beings. The superman can be male or female. Just as mankind goes to describe humans both male and female, superman and supermen should do the same. Supermen are accepting of all beliefs and we do our best to understand how other people feel and will interpret our message. We wish to spread positivity and the value of making yourself the best you can be (a superman). With that in mind, please enjoy this copy of Becoming the Superman. By the end of the book you will have all the tools and determination you need to get everything out of life.

Table of Contents

Introduction - Oh, the Humanity

You're picking up this book because you noticed there is room for growth in your life. Maybe you are unhappy, maybe not. It is likely that you just don't know all of the areas in your life that need improvement. You might want change or you may not realize that change is a possibility for you. It is. I'm glad I have this opportunity to tell you that you've made the right choice if you have purchased this book or even if you're simply reading it in a bookstore, library, or on an e-reader. Congratulations! The first step toward improvement is seeking change and the knowledge of how to change. I can assure you that you have made the right decision in reading this book if you are truly serious about wanting to improve yourself, your life, and the world as a whole. If you follow even one of the steps or a single piece of advice that is offered in this book, your life will be much more rewarding. If you follow all of it, have no doubt that you will no longer be plain old you, the boring normal person going through day to day life wishing for fulfillment. You can be the superman, and don't let anyone else or even yourself try to tell you otherwise.

I would like to start off by explaining to you who the superman is, how he came to be, and what you can do to be the best. If you are already a superman that's great! Supermen know that reestablishing knowledge through activities like reading and following the lessons of this book is something successful people do. There is no limit to how often you learn new things and there is so much to gain, even from materials you have already read, and habits you already practice. You're learning and even more importantly, you are reinforcing the knowledge and message of greatness. The best ways to hold on to this material is to read it on a regular basis, follow the advice and to take notes along the way. The more you think about what you are reading and how it can be implemented in your life, the more of an impact it will have. It takes longer to read a book when taking notes and that was something that would stop me too, until I realized how much more can be gained from the material by taking notes and thinking critically about how to apply it in my life. Even if you no longer have the book you can quickly look through your notes and understand the message in a way that you have tailored to yourself. So if your whole heart is in this and you are serious about making something out of yourself, get out a notebook and be ready to take notes and copy passages that are meaningful, helpful, and best represent the chapter. I am going to tell you right now, you can probably read through this book in one sitting in only a few hours if you speed through it. If you do that you will be lucky if you take anything at all from it. That would be like glancing out your window then shutting the blinds before trying to paint a realistic version of it. Then imagine trying to do that after having glanced out the window last year. You get the point. You have seen the key ideas by speed-reading but if you're not working with them and learning, you will be wasting your time. It's not an accomplishment to read a book; it's an accomplishment to learn from it and apply the message to your day-to-day life. It is an accomplishment to remember what you've learned and practice it decades from now. That will be the difference of saying you've read it and saying it's changed your life.

How I Became the Superman

When I reached 25 years old I started to wonder what it was I was doing with myself. For some of us it takes a life changing event such as a near death experience or hitting rock bottom. The morning I woke up with bruises, covered in mud in my bedroom not knowing how I got there was that point for me. A few years after college I could feel myself slipping. I was gaining weight, had a lesser vocabulary and wasn't taking care of myself. I was sleeping through work because I was out drinking until 2:00 am and doing heaven knows what with girls I just met in places I shouldn't have been. It was at that point I saw myself and was disgusted. I was working three jobs so that I wouldn't have free time to spend gallivanting, but even then I was burning the candle at both ends not only working but misbehaving at all hours of the night. When I reached this realization, I started listening to motivational tapes and reading all of the self-improvement books I could get my hands on. It was hard at first, especially trying to persuade other people that self-help doesn't make you a loser but in fact the opposite. If everyone that needed help improving themselves took to reading with the right motivation, the world would be half way perfect already. So it became my quest. I would become the superman. I stopped going out to bars and cut back on everything that was bad for me. I even sold my television. There were setbacks of course: nights when I couldn't control myself and the few other television sets I had to sell afterward as well. My time suddenly became more valuable to me. I noticed the lost time if I watched a movie or spent time on the internet.

I met a fellow superman (he was the first person I helped) who went to the bar with me. We would go to the bar together but we behaved. We brought ear plugs because of the loud music, drank diet coke, played cards, and went home early. Then we even started playing backgammon. People would stare at us from all over the bar. The servers loved us because we behaved and tipped well. What I saw was envy. Everyone around us wished they could be like we were. They secretly loathed the attachment they had to alcohol. It took two intelligent people to show them that they were wasting their lives. It took being on the other side to show me that I had been wasting my life.

When I wasn't with my friend, I would go out and drink and hate everything about it. I hated the people, I hated what I was doing, I hated the whole atmosphere and the way they exist. It got to the point that I would go out to the bar and not even have a drink, but walk out two minutes later disgusted that people enjoyed that sort of thing. I did that a number of times over a number of months. There was still part of me expecting to find something good there or to at least get away from myself. Now that I was accountable it never felt good. Not before, not during, and not after. I loathed the urges that I had before I got there and finally stopped feeling them when I saw how my perception had changed. I felt like a failure every time I walked to the bar instead of going home to go to sleep. When I was there, I realized I'm nothing like these people. I am going to be so much more than I have been, in fact I already am someone else because of what I now see of this place. I saw other people that were letting the world drag them down. Even worse, they were dragging themselves down. More and more unused and overlooked potential that they were sucking away from every new person that would join them. It aggravated me. I wanted the world to know better.

At this stage I am ready to tell the world, which is why I'm finally writing it down for everyone. I was well on my path and I knew that one day I would become the superman. I was getting there. I woke up early every day and exercised a few more times a week. When I got up in the morning and before I went to sleep at night I would read. While I was driving or taking a shower I would listen to audio books. There was not a moment of waste. Even as I type now I am listening to Symphonie Fantastique by Hector Berlioz and loving it. It is great to be able to appreciate art. **I fill my life with that which will improve me.** Everything starts to look better. Food starts to taste better. Feelings become amplified. People start to like you more. On my days off I cleaned and went hiking in between reading, listening, and working out. I looked at my life and realized it was exhilarating. It felt good in every way. I was making new friends with the same ideals, doing better at work, and seeing who was really an important part of my life and who was trying to drag me down. I was well on my way and I knew that I was going to be the superman.

A short time later I took a three-day seminar on life improvement. I can't say whether the seminar itself was of very much help to me because it was mostly about my relationships with other people which was never an issue. I have a great relationship with my parents and I knew I was improving myself before I went. When I got home the seminar people called me and said, "So, what did the seminar do for you?" It was at that moment that it finally clicked. The most important thing that I took from it was my own personal realization that I was not going to become the superman. I already was the superman. I just needed to act like it and realize my full potential. The woman on the phone must have thought I was nuts. I didn't explain any of it to her, I just told her that I didn't have to become someone else but just start being what I already was and had the potential to be all along. I was no longer striving for something beyond my grasp, I was embracing the path of improvement, the path of the superman. It was from the seminar that I let myself be the superman and it was through attending their program that I realized that everyone has the same potential. It finally spoke out to mc that there is so much potential that people don't know they have. I understood now that I could be the one to encourage and cultivate this inside of all of us. I decided to start writing and to put out this declaration that we shall all be supermen. Everyone that is willing to commit to the changes that follow and be a part of something greater will be a superman and their quality of life will reflect this.

Summary: Recognize that you are not trying to become the superman, you are the superman and you need to start living your life accordingly and acting like it.

Commit to becoming the superman.

Further reading:
"Better Than Good: Creating a Life You Can't Wait to Live" - Zig Ziglar
"See You At the Top" - Zig Ziglar
"How to Stop Worrying and Start Living" - Dale Carnegie

Section I - Who is the Superman?

Chapter 1 – What the Superman is and What the Superman is Not

The idea of the superman has been around for a long time. It has always been someone that we look up to and that we would like to be. It has been misused by those with ill intentions, as some may know, during World War II and after Nietzsche died leaving his work at the will of his sister and her husband who spread hate toward Judaism. Furthermore, supermen are not people from a distant planet who can lift buildings and shoot lasers from their eyes. The real superman prevents the spread of negativity and hate. The superman is accepting of all and does everything possible to help others and himself. The superman is inside of all of us. He is the potential we have to become something more. We are only greater than those that ignore their potential in life and refuse to improve. Change comes only from action. We do not dislike people we cannot help, we feel bad for them and the world they are forcing themselves to live in. We have no enemies. The world is full of people that we can help and the benefit is clear from the start.

As supermen we are dedicated to improving everything about the world. We are dedicated to improving ourselves, our friends and family, our environment, our jobs, and the lives of all of those around us. We are here to show the world that it does not have to accept anything it doesn't, things can be changed. We are here to show everyone that they can be better, feel better, and live better. That they are better and need to start acting like it by ascribing to the super-mentality to create a better world for all of us and for generations to come. We are here to lift everyone up out of their stagnation and their slump of boredom and unproductivity. We want everyone to feel how amazing it is to be better than they knew possible. We want to share the excitement of success and the satisfaction of a life worth living. It starts with us. We must spread the word of success and potential to everyone and create the world we were meant to live in. Spread the message of the supermen and show others what it can create. Be excited about it, **we're shaping the future**!

The superman is possessed by a need for more. It is living our lives to a greater extent than we thought possible. We experience more fun and success because of how we value every moment of our time and what has become fun. Self-improvement is fun. It is impossible not to have fun and feel good when you are improving. There is a whole world out there of improvement waiting for us to experience it and we are ready to let it into our lives and shape our world.

Supermen introspect regularly. They ask others to comment on how they are living life and what changes would be beneficial. Supermen don't take it personally and they use it constructively. They are, in effect, asking for criticism and many times receiving just that. Some people will jump at the chance to criticize, supermen will be thoughtful in their criticism. In the end, it has to be criticism or it will not propagate change. The superman doesn't hear criticism and feel hurt by it, the superman uses it to improve those qualities that were mentioned. The superman does not look for a reason why or why not that person was right or wrong, but simply for what can be done in the future. Supermen ask the person giving the criticism what to do in order to change. The person giving the criticism has the best view of the needed changes because they are watching and are not as associated as you who is blindly acting.

Communicate the super-mentality with others. Do not preach that you are better than anyone else, but that all of us can be better than we are. Supermen encourage others and wish to see people elevated above what they think they can be. As a superman I want to hear my fellow brethren tell me they are better than human, not because of narcissism, but simply because they know we all have that potential and they are living up to it as all of us should. It is a superman that limits or looks down upon others who is truly a lost soul.

We are no better or worse than others by opportunity or simple existence. What makes us better than others is that we not only recognize and strive for our full potential, but that we do all that we can to teach others and elevate them to our position as well. We do not wish to be above anyone else but by forsaking the superman inside of them, others will put themselves down instead of joining us at the top where we were all meant to be.

Further reading:
"Discourses and Selected Writings" - Epictetus and Robert Dobbin
Accelerated Learning - There are a few of these including the original by Colin Rose and newer interpretations by Brian Tracy and a few other authors. There are many books on brain training and memory improvement as well. It's best to skim through and select one that best matches your skill level.
Speed-reading - Any speed reading course will do, most people recognize Evelyn Wood.

Chapter 2 - Ideals

A - The Super-mentality

The super-mentality is described as the constant need and quest for improvement in life physically, mentally, spiritually, and socially. These are the four main categories into which all self-improving activities will fall. The majority of self-improvement activities are mental or physical. It is that much easier to work on the categories we have already spent a lot of time working with. The superman balances the categories and spends the right amount of time for success in each one. Supermen hold the super-mentality when they believe in, encourage and practice all areas of improvement.

[Originally I would have added culturally but it has been ascertained that culture is a sub-category of most of the other categories. Culture is a big part of understanding how other people function in life. It thus allows us to improve socially. In the form of art and other brain stimulating activities (music) it allows us to improve mentally. It also helps us to relax and feel a sense of belonging, which reduces stress in day-to-day life. Spiritually all forms of belief and religion are a part of that culture. There are many different cultures, and to go into specific detail on any one of them would leave the others lacking.]

B - The Super-manifesto

The super-manifesto is to subscribe to the way of life of the superman. It is a call to goal setting and positive habit forming. It is subscribing to the super-mentality and thus improving your life and how you live in every way possible. This is a public declaration that all of us are part of something that will make us bigger and better than we are now. Together we will create this world of supermen by bringing our fellow men up to our level and helping them subscribe to the self-improvement ideology that we follow. Improving your life starts with improving yourself and continues with helping others improve.

All of life is built on ideas and beliefs that you have created and reinforced in your actions, your life, and your mind. We are what we think and what we think comes to be. The past is a major part of what holds us back from furthering our lives. Even the little things that we carry with us from day to day. Life has you distracted from the people who really care about you.

C - Ruling the World

We are rulers of our own world. We were born leaders of everything. It is our responsibility to shape the world into the best world possible. The true ideal of a ruler is to do what's best for everybody. The superman holds the same goal. We start by ruling our own world and in time we are made leaders of the entire world. We accept that we are able to change things larger than ourselves by being supermen. We rule the world because we are always climbing higher than everyone else thought possible. We are not on top to rule over others, but to rule over everything that holds people back from ruling along with us. Our goal is for everybody to be on the same level we are, and constantly striving for more. Each individual makes up the whole of the supermen and by subscribing to this level of life we allow ourselves to rule, and encourage others to rule with us. Ruling alone is unfulfilling. If no one could reach the same level, it is not a level worth reaching. If you can't lift others higher, you're not doing your job as a leader. We are here because we want everyone to reach this level of life and to experience the joy and satisfaction we feel every day in everything we do. Everything is possible, but only if we work together.

Further reading:
"The Psychology of Persuasion: How to Persuade Others to Your Way of Thinking" - Kevin Hogan [Kevin Hogan teaches a win/win or no deal philosophy. Both parties should benefit from every deal or the deal should be cancelled.]
"How to Win Friends and Influence People" - Dale Carnegie

Assignment: Make a List of Your Features

Make two lists, one of what you consider your best features and a second list of features you need to improve upon. At this point look at the second list and instead of saying, I have a problem with or I am no good at what is on the list, change the message to a positive one. Not one of a weakness that needs improvement, but of present success. For example, I am not good at chess or I want to be better at soccer. Change these to I am great at chess, I am great at soccer. I love waking up early, I really enjoy exercising, I eat very little and lose weight without trying. The more specific the better because the easier it is to change. It is hard to be a superman in one area if you are trying to change your understanding as a whole. I am no good at soccer. What makes you no good at soccer? Everything? You can work on that by playing soccer and practicing but as you do that you'll notice that some parts are harder for you than others. I am pretty good at running down the field, I just can't pass the ball very well. This changes it from I am no good at soccer to I'm no good at passing. It is one hundred times easier to improve on passing than it is to get better at soccer as a whole (recognize your weak areas).

In the second list, "I'm no good at soccer," will be changed to, "I'm great at passing the ball." Why are you great at passing the ball? You are because you realize it is not yet your strong suit and you are going to convince yourself that it is. Every day you will spend time passing the ball as often as you can until you are the best at passing the ball. **You will never be great at anything in life if you know you are not great at it.** You can only become great by knowing you are the superman and that it is possible. You are already great at it and the amount of time you spend improving will make you better than great, it will make you the best. There are plenty of people who are naturally great at things, but can never reach the skill level of someone who knows he is great because the amount of time he spends raising himself above greatness will be lower, and the time spent lacking confidence will hinder progress.

Once your second list has been altered to reflect positive facts, add it to your first list so you have one long list of things that make you the superman. A superman knows his strengths and knows that there is no such thing as weakness, only opportunity to improve. The superman works every day to improve not only the things he has not mastered, but to practice and improve the things that he has. The natural who never practices will never achieve greater results than a regular person who practices. If you don't use it, you lose it. Our goal is to find it and cultivate it before it dies. It dies once you accept that it is not possible.

Once you have created your final list you will have your mantra. It may be long and that is okay. You will read this list any time you feel inadequate or feel like something is out of your reach. There is nothing beyond our reach, we are supermen. We rule the world. Reading this list confirms who you are. It removes doubt about who you think you are, and it removes the doubt that you are *going to* do something different. It allows you to do it. It confirms that you are doing it and your actions will follow if you continue to read and re-read this list. You have been programmed your whole life against this list and that is why it was easier for you to think of the second list and things you couldn't do or were not good enough at. It is easy to focus on the negative before you realize the difference. You are there now and your life will show that this new list is the real truth. It is as true as you make it just like your shortcomings were. We surpass shortcomings by not having them. What you believe comes to be, whether it is good or bad. If you think you can, you will. If you think you can't, you won't. Your journey to be the superman is making your skills beyond good and your life and everything you do beyond great. Any time you feel any doubt, read this list and reread it again. Don't just read it, believe it. It is not a list of things you want or don't have, it is a list of facts. It is a list of everything that you do have and that you are. Start acting like it!

You are the superman. We are supermen. We create everything in ourselves and outside of ourselves by helping others create the same thing. Those of us who know we are supermen will always be supermen and nobody else can stop us from being the greatest men on earth. Think about it. The more people in your life that are great and encourage others to be great, the more greatness there will be in the world as a whole. We want to live in a world where everyone is doing everything they can to help everyone. The supermen will always be ahead of everyone else because they know they are and that everyone else can be as well once they embrace the superman they are. Every man has the potential, it is those of us who use it and work beyond it that will become the superman and elevate others to their full potential as well.

Further reading:
Any book by Brian Tracy [His books are extremely useful for all who seek success]
Books on self-talk including, "What to say When you Talk to Yourself" - Shad Helmstetter
Books written by Napoleon Hill including, "Think and Grow Rich."
"The Willpower Instinct" - Kelly McGonigal Ph.D.
"Thinking, Fast and Slow" - Daniel Kahneman

Chapter 3 - Become the Superman

Humans want everyone else to know how they feel. This is selfish. The superman strives to recognize how others feel and wishes to elevate them to his level of living. What we want is a life of peace, serenity, energy, happiness, success and determination. All of these things are within our reach, we just have to take hold of them instead of waiting for them or expecting them to magically appear. People always ask others how they are but they never really want to know the truth. It has become more of a social nicety than an interest in the well being of our fellow man. We openly ridicule our lack of humanity by asking people how they are every day and not caring. People say it to be thoughtful and to be like everyone else. It's all a big satire. Supermen are sincere. The superman asks how you are and the superman wants to know how you are. He wants to make sure you are on the right track toward leading the best possible life you can. That comes from your overall well-being and you should be honest when people are sincere about asking how you are. The superman wants everyone to be as successful as he is and more. The superman wishes to elevate everyone to their highest potential to create a better world for everyone. When a superman says he is fantastic you better believe it. The superman is open and honest about his feelings. He is there to serve mankind so that we may all live a better life.

I won't encourage you to live a life that you are unhappy with. That being said, I do believe you can make your life into a life you want to live. It's actually harder to start over than to recreate and build your current life. People who start over are the ones that are most likely to start over again and again and again until they are out of time. Starting over puts you right back at the beginning again and that's why some people like it. They think they are worse off now than they would be if they were at the very beginning with nothing. This is simply not true. Starting over takes away all of the progress you've been working to make. There are very few times in life when we should choose to start over. There are times and circumstances that demand it, but we should always look at repairing our problems before we look at losing all progress.

Change is part of life. No matter what you do there will be small and large changes throughout your life. You have to expect change now and plan for as much as you can. Your ability to change influences how well you will survive.

Imagine if automobiles never changed. You would be driving down the highway in your Model T at 40 miles per hour. A successful company grows with constant research and development of its product and services to make sure they fit the customer and work better. The best companies stay on top because they always have the latest innovation; that is what makes the difference between their product and their competitor's product. As you should do for yourself. You can't always predict how your life is going to change, but you can control how you react and how prepared you will be to change with life. Would you rather be driving a Model T to work or something built in this century? How you react to change is what determines how happy and successful you will be. If you or anyone you know can't seem to cope with change, then read the book, "Who Moved my Cheese?" The book takes a look at people who are opposed to change and what happens when you get stuck.

Humans teach others that they are great as they are. I appreciate the motive in doing this, to make people feel good about themselves, but in the long run you are hurting them by not encouraging them to be more. These people are great but not as great they can be. "There is always room to grow" should replace "you are perfect as you are." Someone will always be better off than you and someone will always be worse off, but you can control how many are on which side by how much you improve. People could be much greater if they worked hard at being a superman. The inactive superman is as ineffective as everyone else. A man who is not willing to embrace the power he has within to become the greatest will always be an ordinary man. It is sad to see people who don't know what they can accomplish. It hurts me to see people lying to themselves constantly about what they can do in life. It pains me to see people ignore the realization that the world is only as great a place as they make it. The superman will always be on top because the superman never stops improving. The supermen see no limits to what they can become. Supermen see the world and want more. They are the ones who get the most out of life and make dreams come true. Wasted potential is a harsh reality of the modern world.

At a young age we are taught that we can become or do anything in life but somewhere along the way that belief dies. It is smothered by rules and regulations, how you should or shouldn't behave, what you can and can't do. All sorts of limits are placed upon us to stop us from reaching our full potential. Shame on us for accepting this slavery and not challenging oppression. The smartest children are held back and disciplined when they are not offered enough stimulation. They bring everyone down to their level instead of up to ours.

As supermen we transcend the boundaries placed by everything that holds people back. We break through the world of can and can't and choose for ourselves to make the world better for everyone, including ourselves. We want the best out of everything. Nothing will stand in our way. We are the elite few who won't be kept in "our place". We know our place is where we decide it is, not where we are told it is. We will strive and struggle every day with great pleasure to achieve what we want to achieve and to make ourselves into the greatest of all beings. We are aware of what we can be and never limit anything, especially ourselves and our potential. We elevate all of those around us to success through our teaching. Everything is possible and we make it possible together as supermen. Supermen are already out there, all of them, all of us. Do you want to be a man or do you want to be so much more than man is living up to? Do you want to be compared with the lazy, the immoral, the uneducated, the weak, the people who think things are good enough, or do you want to rise above to a higher standard of living? A life where we will never stop improving and rising higher and higher above what society expects of us! You are the superman. You want to be the superman, everything about it speaks directly to your soul that you are not going to waste your life like everyone else. You are living your life to it's fullest because you are the superman!

Chapter 4 - You Are the Superman

Have you ever had to wake up extra early? Was it the hardest thing you've ever had to do or the easiest? It depends on what you told yourself. When I was young I would have to wake up at 3 a.m. to take the early morning flight wherever I was going. It seemed like it was going to be impossible considering all of the days I wouldn't be able to get up before noon. The brain and body are both capable of extraordinary things. The brain is the one thinking about it and most of the time holding you back. The body is just a body, it does what it can do and what you tell it to do. If the body isn't cooperating it's most likely because of what the brain is telling you. They say people can lift cars when fueled with adrenaline. It's times like these when the brain forgets to hold you back and lets the body do the impossible. Your body can do as much as anyone else's. Your brain is an obstacle from getting everything you want out of your body and your life. We influence what is possible every day with what we put in our brains whether it is positive or negative. The goal of the superman is to keep putting in the positive to stay on the right track. **Negative prevents** results from taking place. **Positive allows** infinite results and accomplishment. Negativity closes you off and positivity opens you up.

Going back to the waking up early example. How did I do it? I remember vividly waking up at the time I was supposed to and having enough energy to get myself ready for the day to the airport on time for my flight. I was never late. I planned ahead. When I got in bed at night ready for three hours of sleep, I told my brain what it was going to do and my brain did it. I went to bed and said, "Brain, we're going to get three hours of sleep right now and you have to do your part to get the best sleep you ever have in your life. You are going to use that time wisely and make everything happen that would with eight hours of sleep. I am going to wake up at three, jump out of bed with energy and excitement and conquer my day." You can't just say it, you have to believe it. Your brain will believe it if you do. I have found with this strategy you will have a good five to six hours of energy and accomplishment before you start to get tired. It is likely that you will get tired earlier in the day than normal because you are asking more of your brain and your brain probably isn't used to this if you only do it once in a while. The more often you do it, the more often you will be able to do it. I am not saying to get less sleep than you need, just to occasionally let your brain work miracles for you so that when it does accomplish these wonders you will not see it as a miracle, but as something more commonplace. When the extraordinary becomes average, the impossible becomes extraordinary.

Your body does have it's limits and your brain knows it has limits but like any good parent, your brain looks at the full potential of your body and limits it to what it thinks is the most it should accomplish to be safe. This is very useful if you are living in the wild and don't know where your next meal will come from. Your brain does not want to tire out the body before you can find food. In our lives we do not have that problem but the brain does not yet realize this. If you keep a consistent food schedule your brain will be more wise about this function, but it still has the fear that using too much energy could stop you from getting basic needs.

Say for example your body can do 150 percent. You think it can do 100 percent and your brain lets it do about 70 percent. If you use 120 percent, your body is going to need more time to recover than it did if you use less. Using more than 120 percent does not ordinarily justify the benefits versus loss of having to recover. Once you have convinced yourself and your brain that it can do 100-119 percent efficiently and with ease, you will be that much more productive in your life. The more often you use more than 100 percent, the higher the percentage of what you will be able to do and vice versa. If you do 120 percent on a regular basis, your body will raise from being able to do 150 percent to 151 percent, followed by 152 percent and so on until you have become someone you never knew you could. Your goal is to get the highest percentage possible while still maintaining a healthy lifestyle in the other areas of your life as well. You want to find that critical range that will let you perform optimally. It is best to aim for between 100 and 119 percent. If you aim for more you will achieve more and if you aim for less you will achieve less. If you go too high the recovery time will outweigh the benefits and if you go too low you will not accomplish as much as you can. The reason we set a range is not to limit you, it is both to perform optimally and to let you know that you are doing better and reaching a higher level. Without a low goal you wouldn't know if you were accomplishing anything. Without a high goal you wouldn't know when to slow down in order to perform efficiently. Your high and low goal should both go up with time. You develop a tolerance for this range, which is why it must be made higher as you go along. If the higher number becomes commonplace it is no longer high enough to perform optimally.

On an average day I used to sleep for 10 hours a night and go through the day tired and miserable. I knew this was ridiculous, the brain only needs 8 hours of sleep. It was even worse on those days when I would sleep for 12 hours and feel even worse and have even less energy. I spoke up to my brain and said hey, what are you doing? I know you only need 8 hours to perform optimally and that's what we're going to do from now on. Instead of sleeping from 10 p.m. - 8 a.m., we're going to sleep from 10 p.m. - 6 a.m. and accomplish even more throughout the day. Every day forward when I slept from 10 p.m. – 6 a.m. I would wake up, exercise for an hour and live my day to full satisfaction instead of dragging myself through time waiting for when I would sleep again. I added two waking hours to each day of my life. That is almost 10 percent more of my life that I am living instead of losing it to sleep and not only that, I'm accomplishing more and using the time to feel alive instead of just feeling like I am going through the motions.

Many people will look at studies and say my brain needs more because of my age group or because of this or that. It's only true because they believe it. It's not just sleeping that I'm talking about, it's everything in life that people come up with. It is the last thing I ever want to hear from anyone. These are excuses, people say they are reasons. What is the difference between a reason and an excuse? The difference is you think one is valid when they're both lies. It should make you sick to your stomach when you hear someone else come up with reasons they can't do better. People are incredibly boring with their I can't do this and I can't do that. They can't and they never will be able to because they are convinced of it. We can do it. We are supermen, there is no such thing as can't. Can't is an absurd notion to people who never give up.

You must constantly tell your brain what it can do. Your brain will live up to these expectations if you do.

If you want to shape some part of your life every day repeat the same thing, and tell your brain that you do it and you enjoy doing it. It works for stopping bad habits too. It sounds like it can't be true when you first hear this. Why would something so easy be kept from us? People don't even think about it, it's such an easy thing to do. I didn't believe it when I first heard it but I was determined and I had the willpower to quit. So every time I did what I didn't want to do, I would tell myself I didn't do it and I didn't like doing it. Boy was I surprised when it worked. I knew I had to share it with the world. When I did it I wouldn't enjoy it at all and before I did it I would hesitate because my brain didn't know why I was about to do something it knew I didn't do. It was that easy. After long enough I felt no urge to do it and wouldn't enjoy it if I did. The spell was broken just like that. You're not lying to your brain, you're giving it a goal and if your brain can't reach a goal, nothing in the world can. It is mental programming. You have taught your brain what you can and can't do your whole life and now is the time to reteach it what you desire instead of what the world wanted of you.

Supermen become supermen by doing the things that make them supermen, not just because they can but because they know they can. When the time comes, supermen do these things out of habit without conscious effort as I hope you will one day. We must go to bed as supermen and wake up supermen. We must eat, sleep, and breathe improvement. It should be as big a part of our lives as we can make it. There will no longer be a time when man is simply man. That is a goal we can look forward to.

Take control of your life and yourself. It's not going to be easy. Everything worth having in life doesn't come easily at first. It gets easier over time. Success breeds success. Good habits lead to more good habits. Once you get into a habit you keep that habit until you replace it with another habit. The goal of the superman is to replace all bad habits with good habits. Go from watching television to reading books. Go from drinking alcohol to drinking a protein shake when you work out. Instead of going to bars, go to coffee shops with people that are also improving their lives. Alcoholics Anonymous has it right when they say the best way to stop is to have other people with the same goals support each other. This is true for becoming the superman. The fastest way to become a superman is to do it with other people who have the same goal.

Carry this book around with you and meet other supermen. Create other supermen. Tell everyone you can about how you are making your life the best it can be. You will be surprised how many people are already doing the same. Even when writing this book I told as many people as I could about the ideals and the life of a superman. I couldn't have been more shocked when a young man I only knew for a few hours finished my thought process based on his own beliefs. He said he was determined to improve himself physically, mentally, and spiritually. I started to mention socially as well but he quickly corrected himself adding socially to his list. There are already supermen among us. They are the ones that have the jobs you want, live the life you want to live and have the success you wish you had. I've got news for you my friend, you can have all of these and become this person.

That is why I'm writing this book. I want all of us to be supermen for the good of all mankind. Imagine what the world would be like if everyone was a superman. Everything is easier for everybody else. Everybody supports everybody else. Things get done faster, technology advances rapidly, mortality as a result of unhealthy lifestyles is nearly non-existent, people no longer suffer from depression and anxiety, we are all part of something greater: a society that is constantly developing and improving. Suddenly there is so much more to live for in the world, the development and advancement we could only dream of is within our grasp. The only thing holding us back is ourselves!

We can all be supermen and create a dream world for everyone and future generations. We should bring our children up on self-mastery and teach everyone what is really important in life and how we can all achieve whatever we want. We can finally tell our children they are special and mean it. We can give them confidence and encouragement for what they can be without the emptiness that it usually carries. They will have something to strive for and to achieve just like we do.

Section II - Distractions

Chapter 1 - Eliminate Distractions

Distractions take up a lot of our time. Even if it's not the distraction itself it's something else that came from the distraction that distracted you from your goal. Distractions are hard because they draw attention. They are loud noises, shiny things, and excitement. Anything that takes you away from what is important. They are specifically designed to take your attention without giving you a chance to realize what is happening. The superman recognizes distractions for what they are and gives them the necessary time if they are important and overlooks them altogether if they are not leading toward the goals of the superman. The superman is always on time or early because he allows nothing to be in the way of his goal.

What can hold you back? Anything and everything can if you let it. It's a constant battle if, like many others, you have been programmed into this mindset. **The biggest thing that can hold us back is ourselves** (I can't repeat this enough). We can find any reason in the world or make any little thing into a reason (excuse) not to continue. You might find yourself saying I can't do this because of that. There is no reasonable use of because when it comes to limiting potential. Nothing causes or prevents another thing in the mind of the superman. Nothing is related that you don't think is related. The relation is your creation. It's all in your mind. Because should be seen only as an obstacle to easily dissolve. It shouldn't even be a wall to break through; it should be a realization as soon as you hear yourself say it. I can't blank because... it's not true, I can and there is nothing stopping me beside myself and what I have been programmed to believe. There is no reason for me to stop trying. If something stood in the way when you first tried to do something, you now know what you need to overcome. It's not truly stopping you from doing it until you think it is. Most of the time it is nothing but thinking of or waiting for a reason to give up. Don't let anything stand in your way. When something does stand in your way, don't let it stand there more than once physically and don't let it stand in your way mentally at all or you will really be stuck. If you feel like something is standing in your way, talk to a fellow superman and talk to yourself. Make sure to explain in detail why it is standing in your way and why you haven't figured out how to overcome it yet. I guarantee others will have an answer and once you start being the superman you won't need to talk to anyone else before you come to the answer yourself.

Chapter 2 - Comfort and Satisfaction

Comfort and satisfaction are great. They also hold us back in life. Once comfortable or satisfied most people stop striving for more. This is a grave we have dug ourselves in. Actions and events of the past are just that. The past. We must choose wisely the parts of our past we use to better our lives. Most people use the past as a warning to prevent themselves from making mistakes or taking the risks that would allow them to be free. The man who fails the first time is much less likely to try again than the man who fails the hundredth time, yet they both may have the same skill level and chance of succeeding. Failure was created by man. There is no such thing as failure as we know it. Failure is a lack of change, not a negative change.

Say for example, your car won't start. You don't try once then get out of your car and say my car has failed, it will never work again let's scrap it. The car has not failed to start, it simply hasn't done anything. You are no further from your goal of starting the car at this point. If anything you are closer because if you never try to start it, do you think the car will say that's okay and start itself before you put in the key? You can try to start the car five even six times and still get nothing. Has the car failed? Well, is it still possible that the car will start? Then the car has not failed. Can someone else adjust the car to a point where it will start? Then the car has not failed. It is only when you walk away that there is failure and that is not in the car not starting, it is in you for interpreting that as failure. In our lives things will not work out hundreds of times in many different ways and if you think of each thing that happens as a failure, then you'll never be able to change them. We must be critical in thinking about what is causing this obstacle. In the car example the car did not fail, some part of it was not functioning properly, likely some small thing that could easily be fixed. It's usually the battery, the car may be out of gas, or some other issue that is acting as an obstacle. The same is true in life. We cannot see things as failure but instead should take time to think about what it is that is really holding us back. Once we know it's the battery, we can have a friend help jump-start the car and get right back on the road. Just as we will be able to do in life.

You must recognize now that there will be hard times. If you see something as a failure, do not think that it in any way prevents you from still working and reaching beyond satisfaction; that is part of the super-mentality. We do not blame others for thinking of things as failures but we do blame ourselves for not trying to explain that failure is a man-made illusion used as an excuse to give up.

Chapter 3 - Eliminate Want

Thou shalt not want. You don't need to want anything. Everything that you want is attainable and will follow if you live the life of a superman. Things that seem out of reach because of money, greed, or lust are things that you should be avoiding. The reason everything is attainable is because you know it is and believe it is. Knowing how is ninety percent of the way toward improving. The other part is doing what you have to in order to get there and believing it is possible.

If you are stuck in a cycle of want first write down what it is you want, and then write down what exactly, in every detail possible, you will get out of having what you want. If you can't think of more than one thing, you don't really want it that badly.

Eliminate the things on your list that fall in the negative categories (material goods, people, money). Try to filter the positive things into each one of the categories (mentally, physically, spiritually, socially). Once they are in the categories, balance them into your daily routines until you have what you want so that you're not wanting but obtaining. The superman has no use for want because the superman obtains and achieves. The superman does not just talk about it, the superman makes it happen.

Giving people rewards for doing what they should be doing to live the best life they can is wrong. True rewards come naturally not artificially. Success is more of a reward than any kind of compensation you get in the meantime. This mistake makes people happy for the reward they get instantaneously and not the real reward of enriching and improving their lives. The biggest reward you can ever have is to be the best possible person you can be. Knowing you are improving and going somewhere in life is much more satisfying than a bribe. You will get farther in life than any small reward could ever provide if you live life as a superman. On top of that, people become accustomed to receiving a reward for doing what they should be doing as it is and if they don't continue to get that reward, they will stop working for the real reward. It is a very disturbing situation.

Further reading:
"The Tipping Point: How Little Things Can Make a Difference" - Malcolm Gladwell
"Failing Forward: Turning Mistakes into Stepping Stones for Success" - John C. Maxwell

Chapter 4 - Things to Avoid

I was finding myself saying I hate this and I hate that every time something I didn't like happened, and it started to irritate me. I was insincere on top of being negative! Neither of which I wanted to be. I told myself I was going to say love instead of hate. It took a few tries but now I love it when something bad happens. I hear myself say that and I think why do I love this? Then I remember it's something I can and will overcome. That makes me smile. It is a test I am now passing. It's no longer eating me up inside, I am in control of it. I love it. It feels great. I don't hate anything anymore and I feel a lot better for it. By hating things, those things defeat us. They laugh at you for steaming and stewing and getting stressed out while they are winning. Don't let them win, show them who is in charge. Love them and the struggles they provide you on a day-to-day basis. If there was nothing to overcome, nobody in the world would have achieved anything up to this point. The same is true if they had given up. But there was something to overcome and they didn't give up. They, like the superman, have overcome obstacles and saw that these obstacles were just one more thing they could surpass. So can you. Do it. Feel good about it. It feels good to win. With that being said here is the list of more things to avoid in your life. Stay on the positive side by writing all of the things you can do in life to succeed, but a big part of success is avoiding the things that will hold you back and stop you from getting there sooner.

A - Failure

You are not only achieving great results and success, you are preventing failure. As a superman you will surprise others at how easily you achieve success and that will be mostly because others will see failure where you see failure as not only a lack of change, but a step closer to success and another opportunity to succeed. Preventing failure is as simple as succeeding and not giving up until you have succeeded. Even in the event that something goes the wrong way, it can be a learning experience instead of a failure. This can be the doorway you were looking for, the threshold you need to cross, the burden you need to overcome or that which shows you the way toward victory. Use a lack of success as a guiding light to where you should be going, don't follow failure into the ground, follow its lesson toward success.

B - The Future

The future can be a distraction as well. We look at the future as something that will be here one day and will magically be the way we want it to be without any hard work; if we even think about the future at all. The future may never come, especially your vision of the future. The most you can do is make sure you're on the right track toward the future you are hoping for. There might not be a tomorrow and if there is, we don't know anything about what will take place. We plan an idea shaped by what we believe will happen and what has happened in the past, but it's an educated guess as much as anything else. It is in no way concrete. We like to believe we have control over what happens in our lives. Supermen do. They have control in that they shape the present how they want it thus guiding their future. They don't let anything create the present beside what they choose.

On the same page, nobody plans on getting in a car accident. The superman doesn't either, not just because of how absurd it is; this is merely an example. It could be meeting someone in a bad mood or even rain after a car wash. We predict what we will do throughout the day and what everyone else will do based on what they normally do, but there are so many factors that influence our lives that we never expect. The superman doesn't get stuck on these things, the superman works past them. They are merely obstacles to be surpassed and learned from. In the event of a car accident the superman assesses the situation. The superman makes sure everyone is safe and knows that it will all work out in the end. It's just a car. "It's just" is one of the key phrases of the superman. It puts things into perspective. It's just a car. It's just money. It's just a mindset that I don't have to be stuck in. It's just what it is because it's temporary. It will change. Normal people feel bad about it as long as they want and stew over it whereas the superman is already moving on and accomplishing. Feeling bad about things instead of learning from them is a waste of time and energy. **The superman will always be ahead because of his ability to put things into perspective and realize everything works out in the end.** It was meant to be or it wasn't. It's as simple as that. The superman chooses how to react to any situation and is, therefore, always shaping his own present and future instead of letting the unexpected take over.

We can't choose the things that we don't expect, but a lot of people do just that. They interpret what happened in the past and choose what will happen in the future before it happens. Even worse, they create it in their mind instead of through their daily actions. We create an ideal self in our mind instead of fixing who we are. We make excuses for the past and plans for the future instead of action. Don't wait to be your ideal self, do it right now. We put our ideal self into the past so that we can live with who we've been and the decisions we made. It makes it easier to deal with life. Lying to yourself instead of accepting your mistakes and moving on. It's good to be realistic. We have to learn from our mistakes in order to prevent them in the future. We don't prevent them by forgetting about them or acting like they didn't happen. People who don't take responsibility for their actions are more likely to continue down that path and remain oblivious to how they are shaping their lives and the lives of people around them. Having a blind view of the future with no plan to get there is something that helps people sleep at night. It is not for the superman. The future can be created, but it is only done with precise planning and action in the present. The superman sets clear goals for the future and knows not only where and what the future holds, but how to make the future a reality by living the right life today.

Just as many people shape their memories of themselves unrealistically positive, it's even worse to do the opposite. That is remembering yourself as worse than you really were. Taking credit for other people's mistakes and affirming accusations. People give you a guilt trip about something you did and their constant reference to it shapes how we feel about what we did and who we are. You're not the person you were in the past and you're not the person you are going to be in the future. On top of that you are never what other people say you are, only what you believe. You're you and you're you now. Be anyone you want to be. Just because you were some way in the past doesn't mean you have to be in the future. Be a superman. Be the best possible you there can ever be. Your future is only going to be what you make it through living right now. Don't live in the future and don't live in the past. You are only what you want to be this very moment. Take that to heart and you will always be the superman.

A book that has influenced many lives is, *Be Here Now*. It's as simple as the title suggests. Where are you? Here. When? Now. Pay attention to right now so you can be in control. Don't worry about the rest. Understand that you are where you are right now only and that you'll never be anywhere else but where you are at this time. You don't have to be anywhere else and it's not possible physically, only mentally. When we become nostalgic, we stop moving forward. Living in the past doesn't help you in the present. Whenever you are compelled to worry, take a moment to be where you are instead of being stuck in the future with what you are worrying about. You can't change it by worrying about it. All you can change is how much you get done in life in the meantime. On the same note, put all of your effort into now. Don't hold back or try to save anything for later. Put in your full existence into everything you do and everywhere you are. Don't just exist there, be there, now! Now is all there ever is and it is the only place for shaping reality.

Further reading:
"Steve Jobs" - Walter Isaacson
"Be Here Now" - Ram Dass
"The Power of Now: A Guide to Spiritual Enlightenment" - Eckhart Tolle
"Present Moment Awareness: A Simple Step-by-Step Guide to Living in the Now" - Shannon Duncan
"Everyday Mindfulness - Change Your Life by Living in the Present (Mindfulness for Beginners)" - Jennifer Brooks

C - Phrasing

Life is what you say it is. That can be good or bad. Our goal is to make sure that everything being said is that which will lead to the best possible outcome. Some ideas will be more or less identifiable as positive or negative. Some of these we use every day and do not even realize they are holding us back.

There should be no "what if". What if limits our current circumstances. Instead of dreaming (what if), bring all of the things to a current reality with realistic goals and unrealistic determination. What is stopping "what if" from being a reality? What if I were smarter. I am smarter, I am getting smarter every day through my own effort. What if I tried to accomplish something instead of just thinking about what it would be like to have it? There is a place for what if, but only in our present circumstances. It is okay to say what if when you are ready to try something new. What if I do it this way? It should only be a curious precursor to action. Ingenuity instead of wallowing in what could be. Thinking what if about the past is a waste of time because nothing can change the past besides your own view of it. The only thing that can change the future is the present so instead of thinking "what if", start making it happen! Dreams are only as good as they are realistic and motivating. We should hold off on dreams that are too far from our potential reality because you will lose sight of what is really possible. No dreaming of winning the lottery or having things magically handed to you. It takes up precious time.

I can't do this because of that. It made me sick the first time I heard myself saying it to someone. It took ten seconds for me to turn around my attitude and say wait, that isn't why I'm not doing blank to improve myself; I've had all the opportunity in the world to do blank and I won't act like there is anything but me holding me back. The person even tried to validate my argument (as most people will because sooner or later they will want someone to validate their excuse) but I wouldn't hear it. I told them, I know how it looks but I am not as susceptible as I acted when I first said that, I am in control of everything. I am the superman. Who am I to be held back by anything or anyone else in my life? The superman does not hold himself back with excuses and then pretend to be justified. Your belief that they are stopping you is all that really is holding you back.

It can be very disheartening to try and convince people of this. The super-mentality can be overwhelming and exciting for us but for newcomers it can be met with hesitation and resistance. I had to hold myself back when someone close to me showed that it was apparent there was little interest in what I was communicating. There are people who are stuck and I wish I had time to spend alone with this person to show him that he's so deep into it that he is unwilling to help himself out of it or let anyone else help him. There are people who believe the things holding us back in life are necessary and real. The invisible strings of thought are a thousand times stronger than iron bars when it comes to imprisoning us. People do not realize the hindrance and limitations of that which makes us satisfied with where and who we are. There are people so caught up in what they've been programmed, that it takes a lot more time and attention than any one person has to help them. I have not given up in trying to help him improve, but I have set a goal for him higher than he is ready for. I will take smaller steps in the future because I have heard him tell me he wants success and improvement. He genuinely cares about other people but he has a hard time caring for himself. It is hard to watch people in this situation, which is why I cannot stay idle for long.

I wanted to mention that it won't always be easy when trying to teach. My first step will be to give him a copy of this book, but it is hard to show anyone something they don't want to see. It's even harder to convince yourself of something you don't want to believe. If you run into a brick wall with someone else, don't push them. It's best to let them cool down and you can take a different approach later. People who are stuck in their ways will push back if you push them, that is why we need to take a more gracious approach in trying to help them see what is important. We must also realize that it is not personal. We are not judging these people or ourselves. This is how everyone has been programmed their whole lives and no individual is at fault for following suit. There are people who play an important role in life and it is of importance that we can help them see the truth over time. I believe that we should be able to keep important people in our lives and help them understand. While the superman can accomplish anything alone, it is always easier with help.

Another related issue is what we say in our mind. Talk is cheap but it does shape how we think. Most people refer to this as self-talk. What you say will come to be whether it is good or bad. Our whole lives and beliefs are shaped by what we think and say. Always be positive in speech and believe that you can do anything. Limits you believe in are the only ones that can hold you back and things you believe cannot be changed will not change because of your firm belief.

We encourage supermen to talk to one another about what they are doing, what their goals are and how they are reaching those goals. The superman is not bragging when talking about success, the superman is sharing success and the fact that all of us are achieving it. Success breeds success. Talking about success encourages success in ourselves and others. The superman does not envy his fellow superman because all supermen have the same ability to achieve and enjoy success. The superman does not exaggerate what is possible. Everything is possible. The superman congratulates others in progress and supports them in working toward their next goal.

Now that you know about some of the more troubling negative phrases, here are the positive ones. I can, I will, I am, I do, please, thank you, kind, love, spectacular, fantastic, exciting, awesome, super, of course, my pleasure. Instead of asking why answer yourself why not. We are only held back by that which we believe is holding us back. A lot of this is making our reality what we want it to become by choosing the proper phrasing instead of letting our lives slip into negativity with the programmed phrases that we are accustomed to letting be a part of our lives. At the end of the day our reality is however we perceive it. That is why it's best to keep it positive, determined, and focused on improving. We have this enormous control over our lives that most people don't realize or utilize. We have a choice of good or bad and we do not stop to see that good attracts good and bad attracts bad. We are stuck in negativity with constant complaints, and the feeling that we deserve anything for nothing when we should be doing just the opposite. Compliment others and yourself any chance you get. Make other people feel they are deserving of love and give freely from the heart. Work harder to improve the results you get from your efforts. Everything is within our grasp if we know it is.

D - Money

Money is a harsh reality of our lives. There is so much hatred and loathing toward monetary systems. The evils of money have been preached by many. As Zig Ziglar mentions many times it is not money that is the root of all evil, but the love for money that is the root of all evil. It is the value we place on money and how we put it first in our lives. I believe there are few things of true value and they are as follows: family, faith, people, yourself, perspective, attitude, hard work, improvement, and utilizing creativity. Everything else in life just isn't really important. Essentials like food and shelter will find a way if you are following proper values in your life. We live in a world where this is true, especially with all the handouts being given. True needs for living are no longer what they used to be. Anyone living in America should never have to worry where their next meal is coming from. The new needs for living as a superman are as I have described them.

Ziglar mentions this quote from the bible many times because people often take it out of context. I believe the unconditioned love for anything can be a root of evil. If that weren't true there would be no religious wars. Even a love for God, the greatest reason for goodness in the world, can cause people to kill. Everything we do for the wrong reasons keeps us from moving forward.

We are going to have to live with money throughout our whole lives and this is a normal part of functioning in our society. Don't let money be worth more to you than anything else. Put money in its place and never put it ahead of other people or believe that happiness can be purchased. Happiness comes first from within and second from helping others and yourself. Money is a system of enslavement. It keeps everybody owing somebody else. It puts people into categories making some believe they are better than others.

Love is the opposite in that it provides freedom from social conditioning and categorization. It keeps us focused on what is really important. The problem is that money is the primary source of motivation that our government has to offer. We ascribed value to it and now we must live with it being a commodity that people will fight for and work for. Don't work for money, work for yourself. Work harder because of what you'll gain from it internally, not what will be handed to you with a sense of worth that isn't real. Work harder for the overall sense of satisfaction and fulfillment that comes from what you accomplished. Don't do things just to get paid for them.

You will have to have a job but don't let it feel like you're working for money instead of yourself, your future, and the world as a whole. If you are working just for money ask yourself what it really is you want to do in life and start doing it. You can make money at just about everything if you think hard enough and work hard enough. Do what you love as often as you can and in the meantime improve who you are. Be the best at everything you do.

If you have money, let it work for you. Just about every book on success that I have read or listened to has mentioned saving and investing. It separates us from those who do not have money and are stuck doing things they don't like in order to get it. This is a big part of being successful and making sure your later years are comfortable. Start a retirement account as soon as you have money. Money that sits around is more likely to be spent or lost. Don't let it sit there and stagnate or waste it on material goods, invest it. There are a multitude of books on investing. Start small and keep at it until you have a growing fund in stocks, bonds, real estate, and exchange-traded funds. Diversify your portfolio; don't put all your eggs in one basket is still good advice today.

Most sources advise you save at least 10 percent of your total pay to start and as much as you can above that percentage. When you have 10 percent put aside, make your money work for you by investing. This has been the case since the Richest Man In Babylon was published in 1926 and it has been spoken by the most successful people in history, Zig Ziglar, Brian Tracy, Jim Rohn, and many others. This is because we live in a culture that continually spends more when they earn more. Ten percent is the least you should be saving every month. Make it a goal to save at least 10 percent of your total earnings and then save a larger percentage any time you can. The good thing about investments is that the money is not as readily accessible to spend. It's easier to spend money when it is in your hands or the bank than it is to take it out of a retirement account or the stock market. It is not impossible but can you see yourself selling stock, and transferring it to your bank account just to buy a bigger television? It's not that tempting once it's invested. You want it to be difficult to spend your savings because the more that stands in the way, the less likely it is you are going to spend and end up with nothing. Work hard and save hard.

Any luxury in your life you don't need, get rid of or partake in it less frequently. Especially negative money wasting habits such as smoking, drinking, going to bars, television, cell phones and eating out every night. It's amazing how quickly money can come or go if you have the right attitude about it. The key is never to think of money as happiness. Think of it as something you have to deal with because that's what it is. Money is a burden on all of us. The happiest people in the world never think about money. Let it build over time in your investments and in the meantime spend as little as you can. Ask yourself if you really want whatever it is you are spending money on before you buy it.

Technology is one of the biggest suckers of money that exists today. That may be why it's a good investment in the stock market. I once met a man who owned an iphone, an ipad, an ipod touch, an ipad mini, a macbook pro and a macbook air. I took one look at them and said, "You know what the difference between all of these is don't you?" He said, "Of course this one does this and this one does that" and I said, "No, you know what the biggest difference is don't you?" He said, "All right what is the biggest difference?" I said, "Absolutely nothing. You've purchased what is essentially the same thing six different times. If you went to a restaurant and ordered six different meals for yourself they would think you are nuts. You're only going to eat one! Just like you're only going to use one of those devices for all that you need." It doesn't matter if they're all connected and that you can do it on any of them, the fact remains that you've got that many of one thing in one place. At the very most you only need two. That's one portable device to weigh you down all day and one for your home or office where you will be doing all of your work.

Technology has become a burden. This is a most unfortunate turn of events because something that was invented to make our lives easier, more organized, and more connected has now become something that stops us from doing our jobs and living. Technology is great for what it does offer us in terms of learning and working, but the temptation to waste time and energy is far too great for most people to overcome. I heard that the average person on facebook sees over 2000 posts per month. How many of those posts do you think helped them to do their job better? How many of those posts helped them educate themselves? If those people spent that time learning, improving themselves, and doing business, they would be exponentially more successful in life.

Just like reading the newspaper. It's great to know what's going on in the world but how much of that is going to help you succeed in life? Not very much. None of the negativity in the newspaper will help you either. Realizing and correcting time wasted is on top of the list of self-improvement. Don't let technology rule your life. Take back your time! Your email can wait for you at work where it belongs. Social media can wait, in fact it should keep on waiting! The superman is conscious of wasted time. Social media has provided us with very little benefit for the amount of time we spend using it. Even now, while I sit here typing this book, I am only writing this book. I am not stopping to check my email or to see what people are doing on social media. Accomplishments die because of a lack of focus.

Have you noticed how a lot of successful and wealthy people have a cell phone that is years old? A cell phone that doesn't do half the things that the minimum wage grocery clerk has on his phone? You become more successful by doing what successful people do. Successful people don't play games on their cell phone and they don't waste hours every day on social media sites or texting back and forth to people about nothing. What excuse do I hear from these people? It's fun. It's fun. I can't believe it. Wasting time shouldn't be fun. Failing shouldn't be fun! Wasting time should feel awful, and it does when you are a superman. You could be out there creating something meaningful or making yourself better. How many of his over one thousand patents do you think Thomas Edison would have if he spent his time texting or browsing social media instead of working and focusing on creating?

Don't be distracted by these little useless things that waste so much of our time. You only see productive people make phone calls when it is going to benefit them in some way and accomplish something. I keep my cell phone off most of the time. I tell everyone I want to call my cell phone; I don't want my cell phone to call me. It is up to me and not my phone to decide where my attention goes. I know I will only be productive when I am the one taking control of how my time is spent. Some of the poorest people I have ever met spend outrageous sums of money on a new cell phone every year and a data plan that costs more than their grocery bill. Someone looked at my ancient cell phone and said I bet that costs you a lot to use. I don't know what they were thinking. My cell phone costs less than theirs in both time, money and attention. It costs very little monthly because of the limited features and I haven't paid for the hardware in 8 years. They are paying $500 every year for a new phone and $70 a month for service! Some people say it came free with the contract and I say, "That means it really wasn't *really* free was it?" You just agreed to sell your time and that much money per month.

Calculate how much you make an hour and see how many hours of your life your cell phone costs per month, in just money, (for the moment) not time. At minimum wage with a typical $70 a month plan it would be about 7 hours and that's at $10 an hour, which doesn't factor in taxes or higher/lower minimum wages in other areas. Why spend seven hours of your life every month working to pay for something that is going to waste countless more hours of your life? It truly is disgraceful.

Nobody values their time or the time they spent earning money. Just like cable television. You pay how much of your life toward something that is going to take away more of your time. If they wanted me to have cable television they would have to pay me for it and I still wouldn't watch it! It is in no way helpful to me or my life. I would never pay someone to take away and waste my valuable time. These are opiates for the masses and you my friend, should not be seduced by their false promises. Imagine all of the lifeless people sitting in front of a glowing box for hours at a time. It all comes down to suppressing people and stopping them from spending time on success and thinking for themselves. That's why there are so many successful people that came from nothing and so many failures that could have everything. It's not about being better or having more talent, it's about using time wisely and making it happen through hard work. It always comes down to what you spend your time on.

It occurred to me that you can't own anything. Well, there is only one thing you can own and that is yourself. No matter what is taken away, you will always be left with yourself and that's something you can always use to get everything else. There is no such thing as ownership of anything beside yourself. It's all gone when you die. You just keep paying for it your whole life until then.

You buy a piece of land and continue to pay taxes on it your whole life. Every piece of technology you buy has monthly fees and every product you own will deteriorate over time. My advice is avoid anything that you have to pay for more than once. These are things that suck away success the fastest. The biggest thing you should worry about is buying things that will take up your time. Monthly payments are among the fastest way to have money taken out of your pocket and given to someone else. Just to live we have to pay for car insurance, health insurance, clothing, shelter, and food. We no longer live in the days where someone can be out on his own and be self-sustaining. Believe me, the government and big businesses want it that way. They want you to depend on them because if you are helpless, they are in control. Everybody wants more from you all the time. It's tough, I know. Even at this very moment, I want something from you and that is to make yourself the best. The goal is to cut out as many money and time wasting things from your life as possible. There is always going to be something ready to steal from you, keep an eye out on what those things really are. Keep it to a minimum with things that you think you need and don't be wasteful.

There are plenty of good life changing things you can spend money on to help yourself and other people instead of wasting it on monthly fees and new technology. You can pay for someone's education or save a life by donating to any one of the charities that researches diseases. Think about what would happen if you didn't pay for something you are paying for. What could you do with that money instead that would benefit you and the world around you? **Stop paying for all of the things you don't really need and use your money wisely.** Start with cable television, your cell phone, desserts and snack foods, soda, going out to the movies, internet, social media, email, video games, anything that you really don't need! There is no limit to the positive things you could be spending your time and money on. If you feel anxious without these things get rid of them for that very reason (they are controlling you!), then use your time and money wisely. Talk to your friends in person instead of online. Exercise or read a book instead of sitting on the couch.

I've got news for you. Success is not expensive. Some people look at improvement and see the most expensive options. They see monetary limitations instead of the options that are available to everyone every day. One of the best ways to improve is to listen to other people and ask questions about how they improve themselves. Talking to successful people offers you free knowledge! Throughout this book I write about things you can do to better yourself and most of them will cost nothing at all. The ideology will save you money and create a much better life for you if you follow it. You are not saving money because you love money or even care about it, but because you don't want to have to think about it anymore. Once you are comfortable monetarily you will have removed one of the biggest roadblocks in your life. You will be able to see the world clearly and live freely. Never let money determine what you want to do in life or how you treat people and yourself.

One main thing to remember about money is: **be wise with how you spend and how you save.** Keep spending to a minimum and investing to a maximum. Your whole life is an investment. You invest in yourself for success and other people invest in you for the success of their company and their lives as well. You invest in your friends expecting that they will improve your life by being part of it. Evaluate everything in your life often and make sure that everything you do improves your life and success in a noticeable way. This may mean new friends, a new job and a complete overhaul of how you spend your time. Think of it as a weight being lifted, not as something you are losing. You have to get rid of a lot of things in life (wasteful things) in order to have time for success!

Don't be afraid of success and don't think that success is not an option. Success is a choice. It is a conscious decision you must make if you want to live a fulfilling life. Anybody can be successful if they do the right things and follow the right path toward success. You don't become successful by not doing anything or just sitting there expecting it to happen to you because you are somehow worthy or deserving. Success comes to people who attract it into their lives by doing the right things.

There are countless stories of people who win the lottery and lose all of it just as fast as it came. It's not because that person deserved to be rich or poor, it's because of how they live their life and how they view money. There is an infinitesimal chance that you will have something handed to you at some point in your life without any work being done on your part. If you couldn't get it before, you are probably not going to be able to keep it if that does happen. Wouldn't you rather have the 100 percent guarantee of having something that comes with the proper life style and achievement? You can make yourself successful by doing everything laid out in this book and sticking to it, or you can sit there and wonder why it's not being handed to you for nothing. I hope this material is helping to dissuade you from expecting anything to come to you without work being done. Remember, if you get lucky and something comes to you, it wouldn't last you very long if you live the same lifestyle and mindset as you did before. It is the same old story of teach a man to fish versus giving him a fish. Give a man a fish and he will eat for a day, teach a man to fish and he will eat for a lifetime.

Never be a drain on anyone or anything else. This is most important at work and with friends because that is when it can be hardest to see. What kind of a friend is a drain and hindrance on the success of other friends or on someone who trusted them enough to pay them to work? You must provide a balance for the amount you put into whatever it is you are doing. You will always get back what you put into your life even if it isn't instantaneous. People work for how much they think they are getting paid instead of how much they want to get paid and expect to get more for less. This is unrealistic. Do much more than you get paid for and make sure those responsible for your pay know you are doing it. It's harder and harder in today's world to be rewarded for success instead of the amount of time you've been with the company. Those who want more from you will be willing to pay for it if they know you are capable. In times when your efforts are not recognized, you may need to find a job where it is clear how you can be compensated more for the increased amount of work you do and what other responsibilities you can take on.

The only time in life you get something for nothing is from you. You were given your body, your brain and your mind and you can use them to do anything you want. You are the only one who can make yourself better and the only thing you have to spend on it is time and effort. When you are educating yourself and improving, you are rewarded for that effort. Just as you will move backward for wasting time and effort. If you are not getting smarter and healthier you are getting nowhere. You hear it everywhere: "If you're not moving forward, you're moving backward." Life is all about balance and if you start tipping the scale by putting in more, life will adjust and start giving back more. I guarantee it. The same goes for the opposite. If you take out, there will be less and less to take when you really need it.

Success is for people who work harder than they are compensated for and constantly give back to themselves by improving and working harder. The more you put in the more you get back. It's a simple, easy to understand idea that can make anybody in the world successful. It's so simple that most people overlook it and think that they deserve to get more than they work for, or that they even deserve what they currently get for what little they do. Then they are surprised when someone else replaces them. **Someone else is always willing to do more for less and has a more recent education and a better attitude.** Don't make it easy for them. Stay on top of improving yourself and working as hard as you can at everything you do. That's how the person who is willing to do more for less becomes you and you never have to worry about work again. You become the one achieving success, instead of the one being replaced.

You need to demonstrate your value before someone else is going to be willing to give you a chance for more. You won't get paid for things no one knows you can do and they're not going to know you can do them unless you show them. If there is something you see that can be done but you don't know how, study the topic until you can do it. Why find someone else to do something for you that you can learn to do yourself? If it's at your office, do you think they're going to hire another person to do it, or replace you with someone who can do that and your job? What would you do if you owned the business? Hire the person who needs someone else to solve his problems or the one who can fix them with no assistance? You are capable of everything that everybody else is capable of and more. What it comes down to is knowledge, practice, and experience. They can do it because they took the time to learn how and now they do it. The only reason you can't do it is because you haven't learned how or you haven't tried. Stop waiting for it to occur by chance. Learn everything you need to and more so that you reserve your place at the top with the rest of the supermen. It's going to be a lot harder for someone to take your job if you are doing twice the job you were hired for.

Further reading:
"The Richest Man in Babylon" - George S. Clason
"Acres of Diamonds" - Russell H. Conwell and John Wanamaker
"The Power of Positive Thinking" - Dr. Norman Vincent Peale

E - Technology

"You can see the computer age everywhere but in the productivity statistics." - Robert Solow

We shouldn't have to bribe ourselves to be great. The greatest compensation comes long term. Instant gratification is one of the worst things keeping our kids from appreciating the struggle for success. People can do twice the work in half the time, now they use the other half of the time for whatever they want instead of work. Nothing worth having is a hand out and it never will be. **Everything worth having is worth working for.** The worst people in your life are the ones who want to see you fail. People are infected with jealousy and self-loathing. Every time you accomplish more it makes them jealous; they wish they could have what you have without doing anything to deserve it. They think they would be just as happy in your position even if they don't deserve it. They bask in your failures because it makes them feel like they are less of a failure. They are glad they didn't attempt anything because they don't want to feel like you are feeling and they'll never experience the success you do. It's a horrible condition some people live with and a very sad existence. Supermen encourage success in all others as well as in themselves. They are not concerned with the failures of others, just success and how soon the next accomplishment will be. The success of others shows the superman how rewarding their efforts are. Seeing others give up makes us sad. We know it is possible for everyone and wish they understood. We make sure our fellow supermen never give up. Watching people give up reminds us of how terrible and helpless it is to accept failure.

Call your technology, don't let it call you. As I mentioned with my cell phone, I call upon my technology to help me in life, to improve the amount of work I get done in a certain time and to become more intelligent. I use it to better myself and to accomplish something specific. As I have heard so many times you don't get in your car and start driving before you know where you're going, so why would you get on your device with no intent of accomplishing something? Checking status updates is not a good reason to stop working, studying or improving. Do you think Neil Armstrong would have said hold on, I'm not going to be the first man to walk on the moon until I update my Facebook status? Of course he didn't, even if they had that kind of technology he wouldn't have waited another second to accomplish his goal. Look at everyone in the Olympics or in sports. You don't see them in the middle of the action checking their email. They would be booed off the field. Successful people know the limits of what these devices can do for them and they don't waste time on the rest.

Don't get online to shop around and look at things you could buy, get online to purchase a specific item. It is great that we can buy things online and have them delivered to our door, but it is something that can be easily abused instead of used to save time and money. Just like you don't leave the office to go walk around the mall, you don't accomplish anything by doing it online at work either! The internet is a very tempting distraction and if you can't control yourself, try to stay off of the computer. You know very well that if you wouldn't pay someone to do what you are doing at work, than they shouldn't be paying you to do it either. If you insist on wasting your time waste your own time at home, don't waste the time of the people who are paying you to work.

While we are on the topic of buying things, don't buy anything until you are sure it really can do something to help you achieve your goals. This means forget about decorative items that don't do anything but take up space and look nice. You don't need another rug and you don't need new curtains. You do need to educate yourself. You need to be able to solve tomorrow's problems today. Set aside a budget for used books and educational material. Used books are one of the cheapest things you can get and they are one of the most valuable resources in our lives. You learn from reading books, not from being on Facebook. In the same vein you don't learn anything by reading the wrong books and I will help guidebook choices throughout this book. If you are going to buy something take time to research it first and make sure that owning it is a good choice. Will it cost you more in the long run to buy it? By that I don't mean price, I mean the usage you'll get out of it and the productivity in the time spent using it. Don't buy things that will improve your social life unless it's a gift for someone else and even then don't be wasteful about it. Buy them something useful or just write them a check and put it in a card. If they want to waste it that's up to them, don't be a part of it.

Don't buy anything to replace something that doesn't need to be replaced. Back to the cell phone argument, keep your cell phone until it is completely broken beyond the point where it can be useful to improve your life. My current cell phone is eight years old and it does as much now as it did then. It is even faster than some of the new phones people are using! Buying a new phone would be wasteful. You may see a new chair you like that is on sale. I know sales are especially tempting because you feel like you're getting more on a product even though it shouldn't have been priced so high in the first place. Can you sit comfortably on your old chair? If the answer is yes, then don't buy the new one. It is wasteful.

Things that don't need to be replaced shouldn't be replaced. This holds true at work and in life. Do they fire the people who are working the hardest and getting the most done in lieu of someone who is more pleasing to the eye? Of course not. No successful company would. It would take them time to make that new person half as successful and useful as you are now. Whenever you want to buy something ask yourself if it is replacing something else and if that thing really needs to be replaced. In other words is your new object going to provide you with the same thing that your old one already does? Don't replace anything that doesn't need replacing. Especially if you can fix it for less.

Fixing things yourself is great because it teaches you something new and saves money in the process. Almost anything can be fixed and if it can be done for less money than replacing it, fix it or pay someone to fix it. You can Google how to fix anything and watch a ten minute video on YouTube then have the item perfectly functional just like that and for such little cost. This isn't just the instant-gratification generation, it is the instant-education generation. We need to take advantage of that. If it's something you have to go to engineering school for, then opt to pay someone else if it will cost less than a new one. You can pay yourself by letting that experience teach you how to do something smarter; it stimulates the mind. This kind of experience is invaluable. It improves your problem solving skills and makes it generally easier to understand how things work. If you hire someone to fix it ask them to explain it to you, this is another opportunity to learn something. Even if you don't understand it, your brain will benefit.

Section III - Negativity

Chapter 1 - What is Negativity?

Negativity was created by man. At some point someone decided that they had to convey what not good was, instead of leaving us alone with positivity and neutrality. At the time man did not know that negativity would be one of the most powerful and persuasive parts of existence. It is an epidemic. It spreads fast and soon everyone has it. Failure is created by negativity. Negativity causes everything that is bad in our lives including not wanting to, or not thinking we can, improve ourselves, our lives, the lives of those around us, and the world as a whole. Do not be discouraged. Right now everyone thinks failure is an option and they are the ones who do not get up again. The people who settle instead of trying harder are the ones who truly find failure. The superman does not accept failure, the superman strives toward a goal until it is reached. The superman is not hurt by failure but by lack of effort and not trying to exceed expectations.

Before I was a superman I wondered why negativity had to exist. Why couldn't everything be positive instead? It can be if you're looking at it with the right attitude. All feeling was created by man, not actual existence. You may have seen an animal suffer from something that we would call positive or negative. Yes, they do react to stimulus, but unlike man, they do not hold on to it. The second the stimulus is removed, the feeling is also removed. Man carries the feeling with him long after it is needed. Instead of just knowing something is bad, man will remember what it felt like and bring that feeling back when it is not really present.

Positivity and negativity are our creation and we can rule them as part of our domain. The programming most of us have grown up with makes this hard. We have been taught both poles on many occasions; people use it in order to have control over others. At some point we lost sight of our own power and started to see negative as absolute when it was just something we created. A mind at peace understands this and doesn't let extremes take control. We must see the bigger picture and understand that the more positivity we put in the small parts of life, the more positivity will be in the whole. It is the hardest thing to convince someone who is too deep in negativity that it is of their own choosing and creation. Still others think that just because someone else is being negative that it doesn't have any impact on them or their lives. Letting negativity fester whether it bothers you or not is unacceptable. Show people all there is to be happy about; at the very least we can distract them from the negativity long enough for it to lighten. If we are dedicated we can show others that there is no need for the negativity at all. The world is of our own creation. Understand that all there is now in your mind is of your creation and interpretation. Learn to see when you are interpreting things in a negative way and instead choose to see the positive in it and in life. The more you feel of one thing, the more you will make others feel the same way. Negativity will spread it's harmful ways through you, your friends, your family, your life, and everything you care about until someone says enough and cuts you out of their life. You are the only one who can choose it. You just have to be willing and determined. A half-hearted effort will get you nowhere.

Chapter 2 - Transducing Negativity

Everything negative must be made positive by supermen. Supermen look past negativity and bring positivity to all of those who come in contact with them. It may be as easy as seeing the bigger picture and where the small event fits in. It may not be easy at all. That is okay. Anything that starts off easy usually isn't an accomplishment. Negativity is merely another obstacle and challenge for us to surpass and move on from in life. We must leave it behind and teach others to avoid it as well. A world without negativity sure would be a great place to live wouldn't it? Imagine if everyone in the past who gave up had been more positive and kept trying. It's easier to realize how much is possible when there is no negativity floating around telling you not to try. Always be positive. Everything gets better in time if you have a positive attitude and determination. Remember, everything is possible if you believe it and create it.

Negativity repels positivity and attracts negativity. Negativity sucks positivity out of people and replaces it with angst and depression. Success is created by positivity and the constant effort that comes with believing. Success hangs around with positivity just like failure hangs around with negativity. If one of the two is around, the other is sure to follow. Eliminate it from your vocabulary. Eliminate it from your life. That which you put out will go back in and that which you put in will come back out. Life is created based on the input, output, and interpretation (perspective) of everything around us. Keep it positive and you'll live a happy life. Make a conscious choice to stop accepting negativity. There is no such thing as negative, it is man made yet here it is causing us so much grief. The best way to eliminate negativity from your life is first to recognize it and then to turn it into positivity. Instead of being upset your car broke down be happy that you have a little more time that you can spend outside, a break from the hustle and bustle of your life. On top of that you now get to be a creative thinker and have a situation you can take charge of. Don't let it bring you down, bring yourself up and laugh as negativity floats by thinking it has power over you.

Chapter 3 - Paranoia

Nobody wants you to succeed and nobody wants you to fail. Frankly, they don't think about you as much as you do. They think about themselves not what other people think of them. Supermen wish everyone success. Your fellow supermen want to see you get ahead. They want to see everyone improving and succeeding. They want you to reach a high level of success because it is motivating to see where they can go as well. Supermen that are ahead relive the joy of their success by watching you advance.

Paranoia is narcissistic. The most paranoid people I have met think that everyone in the world is thinking about them all the time. It is a negative and pessimistic attitude to have. An optimist thinks about how happy everyone else must be today because that is how he feels as well. It is of no benefit to imagine that others are out to get you. The news cultivates this belief in every American. There is no getting past 'the world is a terrible place' and 'everyone is out to get you' mentality of the news. It is fear mongering and we as a society eat it up. They wouldn't broadcast it this way if it didn't get the most viewers. It is more true that people have their own agenda in life. There may be people out to get you, but they are mostly doing it accidentally in the process of trying to get what they want.

Supermen know that their success is not dependent on your failure. Large companies end up killing people with things like pollution and redevelopment because they are trying to save money not because they thought of these people and wanted to harm them. Don't get me wrong, ignorance is no excuse. Don't spend your life imagining other people are thinking about you. Even if they are, what concern is it of yours? When you are a superman people will start thinking about you in a positive way because they will admire you and want to be like you. It is your job to notice this and tell them they are supermen too if they want to be. The goal of this is to receive positive attention from others so that you may elevate them to our level of being. The more of us there are working toward one goal of improvement, the easier and happier it will be for everyone. Everybody has the ability to become the superman, there is literally nothing stopping any of them but themselves just as **the only thing that can hold you back is you**!

Assignment: Change Your Negativity

Make a list of all that is negative in your life from the simplest comment you or someone else made about something, someone, or yourself, to something truly challenging that makes it more difficult for us to keep positive. (Someone dying, things that seem too hard to accomplish, disabilities, worry, etc.) If any of it is materialistic, this should be the easiest thing for you to look past in life; that includes not being able to afford something or having something break or not work properly. Once this list is made, promise yourself you will notice when you or someone else is negative in your life (keep adding to the list if it isn't already part of it). Once you start to notice it occurring and either stop yourself or let the other person know that you would prefer not to be a part of anything negative, then you can put a smiley face next to it on your list. Once it happens a few more times and you notice it and start to change it, cross it off your list. Once you do this, then when something you have already gotten over happens, you will smile about it and remember your accomplishment of letting go.

Sometimes the easiest way to change once you notice it is to bring to light something positive instead. Every cloud has a silver lining is what we've been told our whole lives and it is up to the supermen to only see the silver lining and to show it to others as well. I am fortunate enough to live in a state that has mostly sunshine and positive people. It is the only place I've been where everyone starts smiling when it rains if they weren't already smiling from the sunshine. The same thing happens when it snows. It's always so beautiful that when it isn't, that too makes people happy. This is how you should be in your life. Be happy about everything positive then when something you perceive as negative occurs, be happy about it because you're lucky enough to be in a position where this can occur and you have the power to keep it from changing how you feel.

We need to think about this list every day and see if today something happened that needs to be added to the list in order to eliminate negativity from life. By the end of the year you should have very few, if any, negative events on your life. If you still have a lot of it, go back to your list and see where you have not been noticing or making an effort to correct negativity. It's easier to see negativity when we are physically or emotionally hurt by it but it occurs just as often in complaining or even being upset. It should only take you a short amount of time to see it occurring in your life, especially once your list is made and you read it every night. Once everything on the list is crossed out you will be happier and more positive just like that, just like the superman. Don't take it for granted.

Even the superman may have moments of negativity. It is because this assignment has been completed that most supermen will notice it before it happens and stop it in it's tracks. We should keep reviewing the list every night even when it is blank just to make sure that we are not missing something or letting it slowly seep back into us. Don't forget, negativity is draining. If it's not draining your life away it is draining away from someone else. The superman feels this drain of energy and does not wish to be part of what a burden on society it is. Supermen will do all that it takes to stay positive and optimistic in order to make the world a better place for all of us.

Further reading:
"You Can't Afford the Luxury of Negative Thought" - Peter McWilliams
"Positive Words, Powerful Results: Simple Words to Honor, Affirm, and Celebrate Life" - Hal Urban
"Negaholics: How to Overcome Negativity and Turn Your Life Around" - Cherie Carter-Scott
"Feeling Good: The New Mood Therapy" - David D. Burns, M.D.
"Emotional Freedom: Liberate Yourself from Negative Emotions and Transform Your Life" - Judith Orloff

Section IV - Goals

Chapter 1 - Goal Setting

There are a number of levels toward and beyond success. Your goal should always be the next level. Reaching a point of satisfaction keeps us from getting any higher in our quest for improvement. One who does not work toward improvement never will get any higher. There is no level that we cannot reach, there simply is not enough time in life to have that much influence and power over the world. There is a limit to what level we can reach in life but it is only set by effort and time. We do not have any control over time but we do have control over effort. In having goals we form in reality where we will be going and where we want to go. It is impossible to know the highest levels we will reach in life until we are closer to that time. Right now we hypothesize, anticipate and work ever harder to keep rising.

The superman makes plans and sets goals. Success does not come as a surprise to someone who already knows where it is and has been working to get there. Neither should failure if you're ignoring your plan for success. You can never get where you're going if you don't know where that is. For example, when you have to go somewhere you've never been and don't know the address you don't just walk outside and say I'm going to keep walking or driving until I get there. If you make it to that place it will be out of blind luck, but it's more likely that you'll get lost and never find your destination. It will take you that much more time wasted to get back where you started. All of the positivity in the world isn't going to get you somewhere specific. It can get you some place better and unexpected, but it's also more likely that you'll just end up nowhere.

There is only so much time in the day, use it wisely! Everybody says they don't have enough time to do things. You'll find it amazing how much time you really do have but never use. Working a standard 40-hour a week job will leave you with plenty of time to accomplish anything you want. There are 168 hours in a week, subtract 45, that's 40 for working and 5 for commuting and you have 123. Subtract 8 hours a night in sleep (56 for seven days) and then you have 67 free hours. Let's say it takes 2 hours a day (14 per week) to take care of shopping, cleaning and eating. That leaves you with **53 hours to do absolutely anything** you want. That's more than a full time job. That's over two full days every week. Did you know you had all of that time to do whatever you want? It's easy to see on your calendar. Use that space to shape yourself into what you want to be and use it wisely! If you wasted time at work you wouldn't get paid for it, yet here you are wasting your time at home and you are getting nothing out of it when you could be getting everything. Bettering yourself should be your full time job. You can do it not only those 53 hours but every other hour as well. You can learn more and do better at work as well as listen to books on tape while you do other things.

Chapter 2 - Habits

Habits Are Coal We Turn Into Diamonds

What stops change from being easy? Habit and the effort we put in. When you first start a habit it is like carbon. It is weak and breaks easily if you drop it. In time the pressure you put on it from doing it over and over will turn the carbon into diamond. Once a habit is a diamond it is nearly impossible to break. You can drop it a few times and it will still be an integral part of your life. Just like with real diamonds you can't just give them away because people would think you're nuts. You have to sell them and you get something else in return. The best way to sell a habit is to create another habit in it's place. Make that new habit a positive one.

Habit is a big part of life. You need to replace bad habits with good habits and create new habits where there are none. It is easy to lay out the habits you would like to incorporate and also the ones you want to get rid of. It is harder, in practice, to really make or break these habits. You can see all that you want and need to do to improve yourself but often succumb to the negative and time wasting desires of life without proper balance. There are things that are good for you, things that are not good for you and the in between things that are neither conclusively good or bad. The in between things should come in moderation. Things that are not good for you should be limited to as little as possible and the things that are good for you should come into your life slowly at first but gradually rise to more and more (so that they have a firm foundation to build upon). Too much of any of these is bad. Too much of that which is not good for you will kill you. Now and later. Too much of what is good for you usually leads to exhaustion. Too much of the in between things lead to stagnation and general degradation of the mind and body.

Brainstorm good habits. Many people live the best or worst lives they can because of habit. Even worse there are people leading boring lives because of force of habit. The superman understands that habit is the most influential part of life. It becomes what we do most often and, good or bad, is reflected in our life as a whole.

It can be hard at first to change your habits not only because of how deeply they have rooted into your life, but also because they seem to have some sort of perception filter. Some habits are more noticeable than others. We don't want to believe that the bad habits we have are in fact habits instead of just something we do every so often. They are bad habits and you need to realize the control they have over you. Other times it takes everyone in our lives pointing it out until we say gee, maybe I do have a problem. Any time someone tells you there is something you shouldn't do that you do often, write it down on a separate page for your list of good and bad habits. You don't have to believe it's a habit, just humor me. Eventually you'll start to see which ones are having an impact on your life or you won't have a life because of them. You want to keep your list of bad and good habits so that you can keep your habits in check. If you don't know something can be a problem, it's impossible to stop it before it becomes a problem. Keep track of negative things you end up doing (this shouldn't be very many) just to make sure they don't occur more than once a week. If they do, maybe it's time to move it to the list of bad habits instead.

In setting goals in life, you need to establish where you are and where you want to be. Brainstorm ways of getting there, ways of improving your life in all of the facets. List the things that you don't even think are possible. If you don't consider them they have lost all chance of being possible. We didn't land on the moon by thinking it could never be done.
Zig Ziglar pushes for this message in *See you at the Top*. He points out that we create limits in life that don't actually exist. Then everyone takes them as true and never tries to accomplish more. This is one of the biggest messages of the superman; if you strive to be human and don't think you can be more, you never will be. So make your chart right now. After you make the chart set timely goals for when and how you are going to accomplish each one of the things listed, especially the impossible! Update all of this as often as necessary so that you can raise your goals and have something more to look forward to. We set the goal of landing on the moon, then accomplished it and haven't landed a man on any other planet since. They set their goal, reached it, then

stopped. Decades later we're left with a shabby space program with funding that has been cut exponentially. If they had started with the goal of reaching Neptune before any other nation we would be there by now, instead we barely even reach the goal of getting to the moon any more. When was the last time you heard about someone landing on the moon? In all honesty we do have a space program full of people that are constantly striving for more; imagine where they could go if we had an overall goal of more from the beginning and as a nation.

Further reading:
"See you at the Top" - Zig Ziglar
"Goals!" - Brian Tracy
"7 Habits of Highly Effective People" - Stephen Covey
"Making Habits, Breaking Habits" - Jeremy Dean
"Breaking the Habit of Being Yourself: How to Lose Your Mind and Create a New One" - Joe Dispenza
"Rewire" - Richard O'Connor
"Write it Down, Make it Happen" - Henriette Klauser
"Mind Maps" - Michael Taylor

Chapter 3 - Make a Calendar

Utilize a calendar. I recommend Google Calendar for those of you who have internet access everywhere you go. That way your calendar comes with you. If you are still stuck on a cell phone, most of them have calendars that are easy to sync. Keep in mind you need either internet access or cell phone service to use these in multiple places. If you don't have such service (good job!) you can use an old fashioned calendar, the kind that is printed on paper like a book, and carry it around with you.

To see at a glance what you are spending most of your time doing, categorize activities by color. You should see wasted time take less and less space on your calendar every week. Put a smiley face next to the ones that are positive and the things you forgo. Don't forget, everything you do to improve yourself is positive and it always will be. Did you read for an hour? Positive. Did you do a good job at work today? Positive. Did you workout today? Positive. Did you do some gardening today? Positive. I know we're labeling things as positive, but be weary about labeling things negative on your calendar. At the very most you should put a flat face on the negatives :| The reason being is that negativity breeds negativity. Seeing yourself do something negative makes you feel bad and is more likely to lead to you doing it again because of the impact the feeling has on you. Seeing positive things has the same relationship. They make you feel good and you like to feel good so you keep doing them.

Negativity is a whirlpool that pulls you deeper and deeper. Looking down into the whirlpool will lead you to be pulled down into it when you should be looking up toward where you want to be. You look down and you say oh no I looked down, I'm such a terrible person I keep looking down and you program that into your mind. You become what you say you are and you continue to look down more and more because of how bad it makes you feel. You justify it in your mind as that's who you are. It doesn't have to be like that. The superman looks down then looks up and says "Phew, I won't do that again, I'm someone who looks up and overcomes obstacles." Then he lives up to his self-programming.

Acknowledge when you do things that are negative but don't see them as shaping who you are because you're not that person. Tell yourself who you really are and what you are doing to better yourself and it will happen. You create yourself out of your successes not out of your failures.

Chapter 4 - Reach Your Goal Before Continuing

Reach your goal, then raise it. First, set goals that are within reach. If it immediately seems like you can raise the goal because of your progress take heed, wait until you've reached the smaller goal before raising it to the bigger goal. If you miss a goal or neglect a goal it is not logical that you can accomplish a bigger goal in its place. This will lead to frustration. It can also be an endless cycle of setting goals higher and higher because you haven't yet reached the lower one. That just doesn't make sense. You can accomplish the biggest of goals, but you have to accomplish the smaller ones along the way. The guilt associated with missing your goal or using your time for something not as wise will actually lead you to waste time in a similar fashion. You reason that you already did once, so why not again or you couldn't do it once so you won't be able to again. You will see yourself as having failed and make that a mental picture instead of someone who is succeeding.

This is one of our biggest obstacles. Ourselves. If you don't reach your goal or you end up doing something unproductive when you should be improving that is okay! Don't fret about it. Worrying about doing the wrong thing leads us to do it more often than accepting it and moving on. There will be times when you do something wrong. It's not the end of the world until you think it is and let it become your new habit. Expect to miss some of your goals or not to reach them on the first try. If you set them too low and always reach them on the first try you will get bored. When you do miss a goal say it's okay I'm back on track already now that it is over and I can move on.

The truth is that these distractions are not satisfying. They create a desire and your brain gives you signals that these things will make you happy or make you feel better when the truth is that improving yourself feels much better. Who can say they feel as good after working out as they do sitting in front of a television for three hours? Your brain would prefer it didn't have to do as much and that your body didn't have to do as much but this actually leads to depression and stagnation. Mental stimulation as well as exercise make your brain and body stronger. They make you stronger and they make you feel better. They make you better. So the next time you're planning on exercising but end up watching TV take a step back and say okay, I watched TV and I don't feel as good, but now that I am at this point I'm going to get back to my goals. You have to convince yourself of this for it to be effective. It's okay if you just say it at first (without believing it) because if you keep repeating it, your brain will become convinced. If you enjoy whatever time wasting activity you participated in, tell yourself you didn't and that you would much rather have been doing something to improve yourself. You may not believe it now but soon your brain will repeat it back to you that you don't enjoy it and you won't feel the urge as often, or even enjoy it if you do end up in the same situation.

Here they are, hi goals! I've missed you, you make me so happy but I never remember how good you make me feel. Do remember. Your goals make you happy. Reaching those goals makes you happy and the process makes you happy because you are making yourself better like no one else can. Hi goals, I can't wait to reach the next one so I can set them even higher! You are the superman, wasting time doesn't feel good to you but if you do it, let it go as fast as you can or it will continue dragging you down along with it. Wasting time doesn't feel good. It leaves you a sense of "that was all?" and "where did my time go?" Thinking about not feeling good will stress you out and lead to doing more activities that don't feel good. That is why you must wave goodbye to anything that doesn't make you feel good even if you let your brain tell you it was a good idea. It's over. You're still the superman and you're doing everything you can to stay that way.

It is a vicious cycle. I did something wrong which makes me feel bad which takes away my willpower to do something good so I do something wrong which makes me feel worse because I'm still not doing what I need to do and I feel down about it and get depressed and have anxiety and have absolutely no motivation to do anything productive so I waste time and am left unfulfilled and feeling even worse. Anyone who can muster up the strength to do something positive in this cycle will tell you how good it feels. The first time you exercise or the first week you start reading again it comes back to you like a drug. It's euphoric. I'm sure you already know it for yourself if you look back on a time like this. Tell me about your experience. If not tell me what you could have done and what you're going to do next time. If there is something that will improve you that you haven't done in a long time, take the time and do it. I guarantee it will make you feel good. You may be out of breath at first if it's physical, but when you're done and you are relaxing all day afterward you will feel invincible. The superman always feels this way. The superman lives on this feeling because everything in the life of the superman is for the betterment of the world, on top of the satisfaction of being smart and powerful.

Further reading:
"The Willpower Instinct" - Kelly McGonigal Ph.D.

Chapter 5 - Fighting Through Tolerance

The more you succeed the less gratifying success will be. You develop a tolerance for success as you do for everything else in life. This will lead you to take on bigger challenges and strive ever harder to complete bigger and bigger goals. When people see you taking on these challenges and easily defeating the smaller goals you have set out, they will marvel in your success and they will want it to be that easy for them. They will wish they could take on the world the same way you do. It is your job to convince them they can. There is nothing secret or mysterious from your point of view but for them it is like you are moving mountains. We can all move mountains, it is those of us who think we cannot that never will.

I worked at an art gallery for a good amount of time and I cannot tell you how many people that liked to paint and called themselves artists would come in and look at paintings and say, "I could never paint like that." Of course they can never paint like that, they are limiting themselves just by thinking that way. Artists represented at the gallery didn't just come up with the idea one day and start painting masterpieces. They sat down and felt passionate about painting so they painted. They didn't expect to be Van Gogh after one brushstroke. You will never be on top if you see people above you and say, "I'll never get up there." The only thing that made our artists better than them was that our artists knew they were great. They weren't great, but they knew that they were great. This is what put a brush in their hand every day and influenced them to practice painting every day, go to school for years and learn all about painting and every single technique. So after twenty years when our artist painted, of course it was great. Our thoughts become reality. It wasn't because our artist could never be as good as other artists, it was because our artist was already a great artist and he knew that the only thing keeping him from reaching and surpassing the level of other artists was the time and effort he put toward painting. I lament knowing that the people we talked to would never be that great. They have created and accepted this failure for themselves as you do by forgetting you are the superman, and by forgetting to use their time and effort to cultivate it.

Now, this is not to say that tolerance is a bad thing. In fact the opposite. We need tolerance so we keep doing more and working for more of that euphoric feeling that comes from greater hard work and the ensuing success. If it always felt as good as it did the first time, we would just keep doing it that way instead of improving upon it. Then nothing would advance, we would all be satisfied with the minimum. Tolerance can be good, it exists in you for positive things, but it is detrimental if it exists in you for negative things. I also need to mention that we have our goals and don't set them too high because sometimes we will try too hard to reach them which is hard to recover from. If you work for too long or exercise for too long you will be exhausted, but even worse you will crash from the euphoria after a short amount of time and feel awful leading you to be out of commission for a few days. It's better to start slow and lead up to more than to jump for too much, too soon. One day, when I had been running a mile a day I decided to do more, which is good but I didn't limit myself. I ended up ice skating for an hour, running two and a half miles, then biking four miles and wow, I felt great. The problem is I couldn't keep that up and within a few hours it hit me...hard. I felt utterly drained and it took me a few days to recover physically and even mentally. I could have easily avoided that by sticking to my goals and a gradual rise in the difficulty of them. In the long run it is beneficial to move steadily and not take steps that are too big before you are ready for them. I have no doubt that if I had built up to that amount of exercise, it would have come standard to me and left me feeling great.

Assignment: Ready, Set, Goals

Your assignment is to make a list of your goals. Yes, I know you've probably heard it before. I heard it at least fifteen times before I even considered doing it. Don't be like that. You are taking time to read and improve yourself, take the time to get out a piece of paper or even better a notebook and write today, this week, this month, this year, the next five years, the next ten years and farther if you can. Under each one write down what you are doing, what you want to be doing and where you want to be. What are your goals for today, tomorrow, this week, next week, etc...? If you don't know them or have them you will never reach them or even come close. I promise you that. You miss 100 percent of the goals you never set. If you are serious about success start writing. I was in the same position you are and I shrugged it off a countless number of times for a countless number of reasons all of which had no merit whatsoever but so what, no one knew I wasn't doing it. Then I kept hearing it over and over and over and it started to get to me, gee everyone keeps telling me the same thing for so long. I think it's time I listened. Believe me it will change your life. It gives you something to live up to. This is the number one piece of advice given by every speaker on how you can be successful. It wouldn't come from so many sources if it weren't true. I must stress how serious this is, if you are really convinced that this won't help you it might be time to give this book to someone else. Someone who wants to be a superman.

Section V - Obstacles

Chapter 1 - Holding Yourself Back

What is stopping you from being the superman? Everything you think is stopping you will stop you. You and everyone around you with adverse feelings and beliefs are stopping you from reaching your full potential as the superman. It seems redundant for me to even have to say that it is a self-fulfilling prophecy. All of life and what you think dictates reality. If you build it, he will come. The superman that is. Change how you think and how you feel and act in all the right ways and soon you will find yourself seeing the superman in the mirror every day. It will be you if you will it. You can start right now or you may still need time to deprogram yourself into it. I mentioned programming already, it is what holds all of us back. It is everything we've lived, experienced, thought, and been told. All of that, our story, has made us who we are now and dictates everything we think and do. It doesn't have to. That is the biggest realization that the free man can come to. It is the biggest obstacle toward being a superman. It is what separates everyone who is stuck from the ones who have broken free and taken control of everything. I mentioned our story because that is what you'll hear it referred to as in many cases. They tell you that you need to break free of your story. They are right. They tell you that your story is not you and it is not who you are.

Once you realize that your story is just a story you can start being whatever you want to be instead of having to be a certain way because you think your story creates who you are. It's among the best advice in the world. Never feel like you don't have control. The choice is always yours. I already mentioned that in reality all you have is now, the present. You don't have the past and you don't have the future. The past happened and it was there, but it is no longer there. This is the hardest thing for people to hear. They cling to the past like it is creating something meaningful instead of living life now. To keep the past with us all the time is unnecessary, especially when it is holding us back.

What can't you do? It's not true, you can do it. Even if you haven't done it yet or are finding some other reason why you can't. There is no real reason. The more you don't do it and don't try to do it, the more you think you can't do it and the more likely you will be right. Maybe no one has done it before. It will be that much more of an accomplishment once you do it and show that it can be done. Limits are only created by you and your mind. Zig Ziglar refers to the first man to run a four minute mile. The perceived barrier held everyone back from doing it until one man believed that he could and he did. After that many more people did it as well. Once they lost the barrier as well, they were free to accomplish as much as the man who never saw the barrier. As supermen we do not need to be told what we can and can't do. We know we can do anything and we do it.

Chapter 2 - The Lone Superman

Being a superman alone may be a necessity when you first start improving your life. It is not easy to change, especially when you are surrounded by people and circumstances that constantly remind you of the time you could be wasting instead of using productively. When you are just beginning to build yourself it will be even harder to convince others to join you. This is the time that they will test your will more than any other. Before you accomplish anything everyone who is against it will see it as your weakest moment and want to destroy your journey before it is even started. They may have good intentions and even be trying to protect you. This is because they don't know any better. They have not seen the truth and when talking to someone else who is just beginning to be enlightened, they will do all that they can to be right instead of letting the real world exist. They are scared they will lose some part of themselves or their comfortable lives when they should be more scared that they will never outgrow the petty things that they are holding to value now.

Everyone will have to overcome obstacles and lapses in judgment at one time or another. It is possible to be a lone superman but it is one of the hardest things as well. Especially when we are accustomed to being a part of the materialistic world that has not seen what is truly valuable. We have to break free of the image of comfort that we have created because it isn't real. We encourage every superman to surround themselves with other supermen, not just by meeting and encouraging one another but by helping create other supermen. This will be easier and easier as time goes on and you strengthen your relationship to what is real instead of the falsehood created by our non-progressing comfortable lives. Everyone wants to strive to be more and do more. It is up to us to show them that superman is merely a title we have given ourselves as those dedicated to rising above mediocrity and the false limits that society places upon us. There is nothing that can stop us and they will want to be a part of it. Everyone deserves to be a part of it, to feel what it really means to be alive. The world of going to a job we don't love and spending our free time unconscious is over. Nothing could be further from being alive than the escapist life we currently live. You don't have to escape from life, you have to escape from what you have made of it. Real life is always freeing. It is comforting and light. It is a feeling like no other to be free. Coming from a country that was founded on freedom, I must point out the way people are enslaved by society. Some call it the price of freedom. I call it unnecessary. We can be free in any situation as Socrates spoke before drinking the hemlock. We can never truly be enslaved if we see what is real and what is not real. Become the superman by breaking free of what you think you have to believe. Understand that true belief should be freeing you, not creating limits.

Chapter 3 - Other People

Peer pressure. Peer pressure is hard to overcome for a lot of people. As the superman it will not be hard for you. We will be here right by your side any time you feel that you are unable to go on. Don't be afraid to call upon your brethren for help and motivation. At the worst of times pick up this book and remember that you are loved by all of us and it is sad for us to see you in pain or feeling like you are not in control. People don't realize how good it actually feels to do what is right. It's great being the one person taking care of yourself in a room full of people drinking. They envy you. If you don't conform to the pressures they put upon you, you end up being the one with the power, you end up being in control. There is an initial moment where people will ask if you would like to join them, this will be the hardest part for you to say no but it is imperative that you do. Later you will be thankful that you did not give away your freedom at their request. By giving in they have power over you.

As the superman you are the only one in control and you will only remain this way by exerting that control over your decisions. Once we continue this process, you will meet other supermen and the energy emanating from our group will be for the betterment of yourself and society as a whole. You do not have to be afraid of what anyone will think of you or whether or not you will be accepted. We see you as part of the group no matter what choices you make in life as long as you are still dedicated to creating your own life and making it better. If you have a problem with peer pressure that you cannot overcome, find new groups of people to be around. Take courses in asserting yourself and your beliefs. Find other supermen and people that are willing to stay on the right path and hold the same ideals that you do. It's easiest to be the best when everyone around you is doing and encouraging the same.

Say that someone is directly mean to you; there is not a doubt in your head that it was intentional and it is eating you up inside. Take a step back. What is it this person has done and how has it changed who you are in the short and long term? You are giving them permission to make you feel a certain way because of how they acted, and you are accepting their power and control over you, the superman. Does a superman let other people control his thoughts, his feelings, his actions? Of course not. The superman sees what has happened as a chance for positivity. The more negativity you are handed in life, the more you have the chance to create positivity. How can anyone create positivity if there is no negativity to mold? You take this chance for positivity, you do something nice for that person and you bring up how you felt. Ask the person if something is troubling them. Supermen do not hold back, we better the world by understanding how others feel and make sure that it is as good as we feel. Appreciate comfort and appreciate satisfaction but always strive for greater comfort and greater satisfaction which can only be done by striving for more. Set new goals, reach new goals, repeat. The greater your satisfaction with yourself the easier it will be to stop trying for more but the more necessary it will be. Achievement is the best drug in the world and greater and greater achievement makes you feel better and better. Keep setting higher goals and reaching for more. You are reading this because you want more; never stop wanting more because when you stop wanting more, you stop getting it.

Chapter 4 - Overcoming the Self

We must take the focus away from the "I" once we are secure with our position in life improvement. The path starts within and grows beyond to those around us once we have reached the next level of our path. At some point we realize that there is no I. What we think of as ourselves is the same being in blindness that we think of when we see our lives. It is something that we are comforted by that leads us to feel good or bad. We don't have to feel bad. These feelings are part of a world that doesn't really exist in the same way that the past doesn't exist now. They are a remnant of a time when we needed these feelings to survive and they now limit us. Our goal is to stop being obsessed with the "I" that every sentence is about.

The superman does not bore you to death with talk about I. The superman talks about us and about you. He makes others feel important. Cultivating that sense of I that other people have will make them feel good. As a superman you shouldn't need it because the real you is only what is existing in the present, this very moment thinking and in control. The superman knows that everyone else is important. Everyone else is shaping the world into what it is now, whereas he is shaping it into what it is going to be and he wishes to encourage others to join him in order to do the same. Along with everyone else the superman has meaning; by himself the superman may be lost in his contribution. The more supermen we can create in our lives the more success and development there will be in the world. The goal starts with all of us, especially the I that we are no longer seeing. It is us. We are the supermen. For it is only when we stop thinking of ourselves and start thinking about everything as a whole that we will be united.

Section VI - Improvement

Spend all of your time getting better, stronger, faster, smarter. The main concept of improvement is improving. This can be done mentally, physically, socially, and spiritually. Some areas of improvement are easier than others. The superman works in all of these areas, specializing in the ones that are harder in order to constantly grow and maintain a well-balanced life. The reason being, what is your mind if you are unhealthy, what is your health if you don't like living and what good is any of it if you aren't making a difference? The superman is not wasteful. Everything the superman chooses to do is for the benefit of himself and those around him. The true superman will be self-sacrificing, choosing the benefit of others over himself which will in turn lead to the benefit of the superman. This is not giving in to negativity, but doing only that which will truly benefit the world. Our bodies and minds are the only things we have full control over. We must push them to be the best they can be in order to grow and change the world. Change comes from within and spreads fast.

-Mentally
-Physically
-Socially
-Spiritually

Push yourself as hard as you can to exceed but do not push yourself too hard. You must know your limits but also know that your limits are beyond where you think they are. You must not injure yourself by trying to do something that has not been lead up to by past action. You don't start by lifting a car over your head, you start by lifting something light then progressively adding weight until you are at the point where a car is next in line. This process can be gradual but will most likely be faster than you expect. We already have an idea of what we are capable of and it is both helpful and limiting. Take your limits as a starting place, not a line you cannot cross. Start with this idea of yourself and do more from there reaching further toward full potential and building upon current skill level.

Chapter 1 - Mentally

A - The Most Important of the Big Four

The greatest thing you can do for yourself is cultivating your mind. This comes from reading, receptiveness, environment, creativity and craving more. Once you get a taste of it, you will wonder how you didn't notice it missing from your life.

Technology always advances. We miss a lot of the advancements because they don't always become popular enough for us to hear about them. The internet is nice because it never lets us miss a step. Sure enough anything new that comes to exist will be offered to you for purchase at one point or another online. One of the biggest suppliers of new technology is amazon (not to mention ebay who unites the whole world and allows people in China and Japan to sell you things you didn't know existed for one tenth the price). What I am alluding to here is bluetooth technology. All of us have it on our cell phones, but very few people use it because they fear how they will look in public wearing a headset walking down the street talking to themselves. I've even heard people say they were afraid of the radio waves that bluetooth puts out and that they could damage our thinking. Well take a look around you. There are radio waves from everything these days, especially cell phones and wireless networks. Even using your microwave can interfere with your bluetooth device. I know they aren't exactly "radio" waves but that's an easy way to refer to them. Here is another thing you may not have known: it is illegal to block these signals. What long-term effects could they have?

The beauty of bluetooth technology is that you can listen to audio nearly everywhere. This isn't just to make phone calls, you can buy a transmitter to send any kind of signal to a set of speakers or headphones.

What I want to say is that you can listen to audiobooks at any time, anywhere when you don't have something else to do and sometimes when you do. It's not just great because of the lack of wires all around your house that would get in the way of your hands if attached to headphones. It's about being able to listen to audio books to learn and better yourself at all of those times when you thought you were just doing what you had to and there was no way you could use any of that time wisely. They make wireless bluetooth shower speakers so you can listen to informational and encouraging audiobooks while you are in the shower! You could even listen to your favorite symphony or album while you are showering in order to relax or get ready for the coming day.

What you do in the morning prepares you for the whole day and shapes how your body and mind will act. Doing educational things in the morning gets your mind primed for the whole day. Exercising in the morning gets your body primed for the whole day. Think of yourself as a car. Eating and bathing is like filling it up with gas and getting a car wash. Every so often we have to go to a mechanic/doctor who fixes us and they both tell us that with maintenance we won't have to see them as often. So why not maintain yourself every day instead of just once in a while? You can avoid the mechanic by taking care of your car and you can avoid the doctor by taking care of yourself. Listening to audiobooks in the shower, while you are getting ready in the morning, in transit to work, cleaning around the house, and while running errands, are all personal maintenance.

Exercising is the same. Everything you do in the morning to prepare yourself will keep your brain and body in that mindset for the whole day. Exercising in the morning keeps your resting heart rate down all day. Reading in the morning makes it easier for you to think throughout the day. Your car will seldom break down if you are constantly working on it and making all the needed adjustments to make it run smoothly. Just like with your car, if you don't take care of yourself you will pay more in the long run. You won't get far in life without taking care of yourself and improving. Nothing gets better without something to make it better. Especially people. Like every great leader says, "If you're not moving forward you're moving backward." Even standing still is slowly moving you backward because of all the time you just missed and the age old saying, "use it or lose it."

Reading is the best thing you can do to cultivate your mind. It is the most direct stimulation of the brain along with creative activities. Over time you will learn to improve your focus and mental alertness. Meditation is a good way to enhance your attention span as well. Even exercise helps your focus.

There is an ideal mindset, environment, and physical condition for reading. If you are too tired or too alert your attention span will be either too low or too high. From falling asleep or feeling like you're going to burst if you don't keep moving! Cultivate your condition until it is perfect for reading. At that point, pick something you like (this should be something that helps you learn), then get comfortable and start reading. The environment around you is important in that it should have no distractions. Classical music or smooth jazz is okay but if you find yourself paying attention to anything beside the book, evaluate what is distracting you and how you can keep it out of your way. You may even find that it's the book, in which case you should choose something else to read. **Willingness and receptiveness to what you are doing will make it ten times more beneficial.**

Everyone can tell you that doing something you want to do is so much easier than doing something you don't want to do. You are reading this book because you want to take those bad habits and swap them with all of the self-improvement you know you need. I want you to want every part of a better lifestyle. I want you to stop wanting all of the bad distracting things in your life and start wanting what will make you feel the best and be the most successful. Some people would kill to be that person, yet they won't get up off the couch or make the effort. You are better than that, you have already gotten this far in learning what to do and I pray you have already started taking the steps I have laid out and made progress.

If you insist that you are not someone that likes reading then ask yourself this question. Do you like getting better and smarter? When we get sick the only thing in the world that we want is to get better, yet here we are suffering from a less obvious sickness and we ignore it completely. If you could feel this the same way you feel it when you have the flu, you would be the superman in a few hours because you wouldn't want to feel that way. Once you make all of this a part of your lifestyle you will start to feel sick when you don't get your improvement time for the day. You finally realize what you are missing. You start to crave it, just like you want to feel better when you are sick. I know that everybody is interested in something, if it's just self-improvement read all of the books I have recommended so far and the ones they recommend and so on and so forth. It doesn't have to end. There is no limit to how much you can learn and know in life. The only limit is the amount of time spent doing it. Make sure to read something that you like that will benefit you. It's okay to start small. Start with fifteen minutes a day then double it and double that and eventually you'll be sitting with a book instead of sitting in front of a television or computer numbing your brain. If you're always on the go, invest in books on tape. The best self-improvement series are available both in book form and as audiobooks. Some will be better than others but that's how it goes. Even the worst book you read will get you farther than the book that you didn't read.

If you are still having trouble getting started (there are millions of books, I know), here is a list of topics that you should research to improve upon. Just type them into the books section on amazon and read the reviews of each book until you find the one people recommend the highest. It will probably be the one that has been printed the most amount of times and subsequently the lowest price. Each one of the following can be typed into a search engine or book section on any website to bring up a multitude of resources and books you can read to better yourself. Each one will lead to a few others that people have bought as well and show you topics that are similar.

Accelerated learning techniques
The power of the present moment (Be Here Now)
Time management
Public speech/speaking
Memory techniques
Empowerment
Super learning
Self-talk
Having the right attitude
Winning
Relationships

Sympathy
How people think
The Art of Persuasion
Any topic you are interested in and want to learn more about
Investing
Stock market
Philosophy
Love
Meditation
Success
Empathy
Religion
Eating healthy
Cookbooks
Gardening
Zen
Tips for working out
Tips for any subject you want to learn more about
How to earn more
How to be successful
Habit forming
Anything by Brian Tracy or Zig Ziglar
7 Habits - Stephen Covey
Grammar
Languages
Typing
Biographies of successful people
Anything by Dale Carnegie
"Swimming With the Sharks" – Harvey B. Mackay
Any "how to" for business/corporate culture
Anything spiritual you may be interested in - enlightenment, other cultures/religions, and even your own religion (It is amazing how many of us forget and neglect our own beliefs).

The need to be greater is what helps us thrive as a nation and a civilization. That which changes and improves never ends. The supermen will always exist in our world and they will always be the ones at the top. They will always be the leaders and the ones who truly make the world what it is and what it has the potential to be. As supermen we always need to be better, know more, and do better. This is why we are so successful.

Get online right now and find five to ten books that are only four dollars with shipping and can improve you and your life. You can find them on amazon or abebooks. Narrow it down to the best ones and order them. Start reading them as soon as you can and see the results that follow. You can't get better at anything by ignoring it instead of practicing. A refresher will help you perform better as well. The superman never stops improving.

B - Creativity

Take time to be creative in a way of your choosing and be sure to choose wisely. Make it something useful for every living person, not just a sub-group. Art, music, writing, things that can benefit mankind as a whole not just yourself. Creativity is all we have in life, that is, to create something beyond ourselves. By that I mean after hundreds of years what will be left? Some people are concerned with this, others don't even think about it. It's okay to be on either side of it but if you could, wouldn't you rather people remembered you, and for something good? Here it is. Creativity. There is no guarantee that whatever you create will be here in one hundred years or more but I can guarantee it won't be if you don't create it in your lifetime.

For some people it can be a business, family, or legacy. That's a good start but don't forget there are plenty of people spreading their genes all over the world without very much to show for it. You have no control over your family after you leave the planet. To put it bluntly, you won't get very much recognition for it anyway. People rarely point back to the beginning of a bloodline and say wow, thanks so much for having kids four generations ago! In short, passing on your DNA is neither a stable way of being remembered or a really lasting one. Even if your ancestors do remember you, why will anyone else care? We want to be able to help the most people for the longest amount of time by spreading our message and creating. Take a second now to thank your ancestors for whatever choices they made that lead to you being here.

Thank you ancestors, you never could have predicted what has been created. Even at this point we have no idea who our ancestors are past a few generations. The point is that it doesn't amount to anything solid. Businesses fail and get transferred in ownership constantly and bloodlines run out as well as the funds amassed by successful people who leave them to charity and offspring that don't know how to make it grow. Another reason I want you to be creative today is because it will come in handy throughout your whole life in other situations. Improving upon your creativity will build skills that are valuable in most jobs. This includes problem solving, which is one of the biggest areas that determines your success with every company you wish to advance in. Now, back to what you can do to be creative. There are a number of things you can do in order to stimulate creativity right now.

Learn something new. You will find yourself strangely compelled and motivated by this new subject in your life. If it is something of benefit that can help you in the long run; ideally it is something new. Most people have something in their life they wish they had done or wish they could do. Now is your chance. Brainstorm what that thing is that you always wanted to be able to do and start doing it. There is still time while you're alive to do everything you want. Don't think of it as unreachable or silly, write down what you have to do to achieve this new activity in your life and share it with others who are willing to help you along the way. You are on your first step already. If you don't know what there is in life that you think you would enjoy doing, take time to brainstorm and talk to other people about things they enjoy doing. Everyone in the world wants someone else to be able to share the things they enjoy.

If it comes down to absolutely nothing, be one of those people who share what they enjoy with other people. Teach your friend, loved one, or fellow superman something that you already enjoy doing. Chances are they will enjoy it too and even have something in their life they would like to share with you. The true superman not only learns, but also teaches. If you can still find anything standing in your way to stop you from doing this, remember that all of these are excuses and that you are the only one standing in the way of becoming a superman. Normal people find reasons and excuses why they can't do something. The superman recognizes this and recognizes when they fall prey to this life-halting habit. Remember, look for the key words (can't, because, if, will, when, wish, want) and eliminate them from your vocabulary.

C - Things You Can Do to be More Creative

[1] A basic search on amazon has left me with eight free kindle books on how to be creative. This is a simple and easy way to be more creative. Simply buy a book on creativity. It may have some of the same advice I do, hopefully it will have a lot more if it's in a specialized subject instead of the more broad topic of everything you can do to become the superman. My first choice in books from amazon beside the free kindle books would be Creativity by Matthew Fox. The reasoning is simply that you can get it used for $4.00 with shipping and it has good reviews. Having read the reviews I should also mention it does involve God so if that is unappealing to you, keep looking. My second choice is The Accidental Creative by Todd Henry. It has great reviews from a number of people and is under $10 used. By reading the reviews I have also found that he does podcasts as well so that is something to take a look into in order to learn more if I didn't read the book. Even from seeing what amazon recommends as being similar I have found Die Empty: Unleash Your Best Work Every Day also by Todd Henry. Reviews mention that they like it even more than his other book and that it is all about getting past everything that holds us from being great. Sounds like something I would read and reread. One really hard part of being the superman is keeping it up.

[2] Find a simple method to increase your brain function. You will find these in such books as *Brainfit* by Corinne Gediman and *Keep Your Brain Alive* by Manning Rubin. The purpose of these books is to do things that will stimulate your brain in as many different areas as possible. This involves reading, word puzzles, speaking, singing, dancing, repetition, and other brain activities that will keep your brain happy, fresh and renewed.

One of the major lessons they teach you is that when reinforcement routes in the brain stagnate, it doesn't help stimulate the brain as much as doing something new. The big lesson is to do things you would normally do but differently. Drive a different way to work as often as possible, see new areas, think about new ideas, brush your teeth with the opposite hand, see if you can identify things by smell, and tie your shoes a different way.

[3] This one is among the easiest and least expensive: Google it. I did a search five seconds ago, "what can I do to be creative?" It came up with more results than I could look at in a lifetime. Look at every link on the first page and follow the advice they give you! There are many websites on creative ideas you can do and some have over 1,400 images of things that are creative and fun. It will take some creativity and problem solving just to figure out what some of them are based on the pictures.

[4] The fourth way to be creative, and this is the best one, is to practice. Find your creativity zone and stay in it. You may feel like you have very little creativity before you start. So many times you do it with little result, but after time you will do more and more and it will flow easily. If you are an artist keep drawing and keep painting. If you are a writer keep writing. If you are a scientist experiment and write down potential things you can experiment with later. If you like cooking, cook something new. Try to remember the key ingredients to certain types of food so you can eventually make your own without a recipe. If you play an instrument write a song or melody. Experiment!

As a writer I put down all of my ideas and can come back to them at any time to elaborate upon them and create entire worlds from my imagination. Sometimes it even comes down to brainstorming what you can do to improve any part of your life from work to home to personal development. Creating life plans for yourself is stimulating and fun. Have a set amount of time to specifically be creative during your day and use that time to do whatever it is you enjoy doing that is creative. There are so many options here. If you are completely lost with creativity and still can't figure out how you are a creative individual, pick yourself up and start trying different creative activities until one fits. You might end up with cartography or haberdashery but you will find the right fit if you keep trying different things. If you are lucky it will fit in with what you do for a living, which will make it that much easier to be the best.

Some fun things you can do to be creative: Learn to tie different knots. This is especially fun if you wear a tie and it only takes a few minutes a day. Draw or paint anything. You can do it from a template or from your mind. Keep at it and one day you'll be an artist. Keep a journal/diary. If you write about your day every day you will not only become a better writer and better at expressing yourself, you will also help reduce stress. Then when you are a successful superman at the age of 92 you can publish your journal as the memoirs of a great man. Hide things from yourself. This one might not be as fun if you are not open to it. You could move things to different drawers or cabinets in the kitchen. This will help you build new retrieval routes in your brain and help you laugh at yourself. Brainstorming and listing your goals will kill two birds with one stone. You stimulate your mind, creativity and ensure your success in life.

Remember, nothing comes from inaction. Einstein didn't theorize that for every inaction there is an action. The fact is without something there is nothing else. Everything you do comes back to you. Something bad that you do means something bad happens to you. Something you don't do means nothing for you. Something good that you do means something good comes back to you. Which one sounds the most rewarding?

Always do something useful before you go to bed. By this I mean mentally, socially, spiritually, or working on your goals and calendar just like you did when you woke up. The reason I didn't mention physically is that exercising before bed usually keeps you awake. The chemicals released in your brain and body excite your system and make it harder for you to sleep. Exercise is meant to get your heart rate up and it will keep it there for a while when you're trying to get to sleep.

Stretching is good but don't do anything strenuous. The best thing you can do is read. Another good thing is to talk to your partner, your family, or a loved one. Especially your children. Read your children bedtime stories or just listen to them talk about their lives. This is valuable parenting time you can't get back. You can read in your head or you can read out loud to develop different parts of your brain. No matter how you do it, read with the proper lighting and your brain will be ready for sleep when you are done. Make sure to have an environment that is conducive to sleeping (no noise, no light, slightly chilled air). Just like a computer, your brain will not be as productive if it is overheating. It's good to have a window open if you do not have air conditioning. Air conditioning works great too, keep it from sixty-eight to seventy-two degrees Fahrenheit while you sleep.

Chapter 2 - Physically

A - Exercise

Exercising is the best thing you can do for your body on top of eating right. One great thing you should do: walk. Anywhere you need to go that you can walk (within two miles if you are new to it) walk there every day instead of driving (as long as you are in a safe neighborhood)! This is especially useful if it is something you do every day. Think of the gas you will save, the stress of traffic, and the wear on your car but overall think of the benefit to your body. The time it takes to walk is great for listening to audiobooks as well. Make exercise a habit; even small amounts of exercise repeated daily will end up making a huge difference over time. This can be as simple as stretching every morning, lifting weights for ten minutes or so and doing pushups before you take a shower. Try running as well. If your body can handle it, run whenever you can or a few times a week in a safe environment (treadmill at the gym).

One great way to exercise is hiking. It shows you that exercise can be fun and enjoyable as well as let you enjoy nature and get out of the house. I look forward to a great hike every week. One great thing about it is that when you get tired you will only be halfway done because you still have to go all the way back to your car. Try to avoid going around a short trail once and then leaving. If you aren't sweaty and smelly by the time you are done, you haven't done very much. Your body excretes toxins in sweat which means there is that much more toxic material in your body if you don't exercise regularly. There are plenty of books on proper exercise but I also recommend hiring a personal trainer at the gym if you can't find a proper routine on your own. A good place to start is the book *Health* by Ace McCloud, or the exercise and fitness section of any bookstore in person or online.

B - Cleanliness

I can't stress cleanliness enough. Every book on self-improvement mentions it at some point. I'll be reading through a book or half way through an audio program before it comes up and I say yep, there it is. Cleanliness. Cleanliness makes you appealing in all of the five senses though I seriously doubt people will taste you on a daily basis. People don't want to be around someone who isn't clean. Why should they? Do you? It's an assault to their senses. Sometimes I can smell people for up to ten minutes after they leave my office and it gives a lasting impression whether it is negative or positive. It's best if it makes me want more of it (a gentle intriguing fragrance). It's not at all pleasing if I am praying the person will leave my office sooner because it smells like somebody put a rotting corpse on a chair three feet away from me and they keep getting closer breathing in your space. There are plenty of books out there on how to keep yourself clean and I don't mean from drugs though that is part of this as well if you don't have the sense to do so. You should ask a few people in your life sincerely if there is any hygiene of yours that you can improve upon. Most people don't realize they smell and it usually takes a lot of convincing before they'll listen.

Drugs are one thing that keep your body from being clean. People can smell your body excreting toxins well after you stopped taking them. Just ask anyone with an interlock in his or her car. You can't start it after a night of drinking well into the next day. People may not always notice it or point it out to you but it's in the air and it is in no way pleasing. When I was younger I used to wake up, shower, eat breakfast and brush my teeth in the morning and my boss would still ask me, "Have you been drinking?" I hadn't been for at least 9 hours and here it was being noticed. It disgusted me that people could tell that easily. These things infect your body, they infect your life and they infect your soul. Start by removing drugs from your life, (garbage in, garbage out) and taking a shower every day in the morning (so you are clean throughout the day while you are around people, not clean in bed alone all night). Bathe regularly; wash any part of you throughout the day that needs it (most people like to wash their face at night and their hands throughout the day). Wash your hands throughout the day and you will start to notice when they need it. Your hands will start to feel unclean when they aren't clean instead of seeming like they are fine then staining something white because you didn't know you had dirt on them. It is not always visible to the naked eye. You need a sense of what clean is so that you can maintain it. Brush your teeth after eating, floss, and use mouthwash, look in the mirror to make sure you didn't miss something in your teeth. Keep your hair well trimmed and orderly. Shave or trim body hair that provides breeding grounds for odor causing bacteria every day. Find a nice fragrance that is lasting but not overpowering and wear it gently. A little goes a long way and you get what you pay for. Off brands will not smell as good and won't last as long.

Dress for success. Don't dress like anyone you wouldn't want to do business with. Books on this are more than readily available everywhere. Having bad hygiene or not dressing properly should be the least of your worries and are the easiest things that you can fix to get ahead. Practice how you speak and make sure it is pleasant. Ask others around you if there is anything you can do to improve your speaking voice both in everyday conversation and during presentations. Now some of you may be thinking I forgot touch. I didn't. Make sure all gestures and touches you use have a purpose and are comfortable for the people you are using them on and with. Again, ask your friends and colleagues to give you advice on how you use touch to your advantage. There are plenty of books about this as well. It is also what people feel when they touch you. Are they touching something cold, hot, soft, firm, wet or dry? These are all things that can be pleasing or not to the other person. Ask people around you for advice and evaluation and help them in the same fashion. One of the easiest ways to stay cleaner is to lose weight. By exercising your body cleans itself. You excrete toxins throughout the day as mentioned above. Wouldn't you rather exercise and get out the toxins so that throughout the day you aren't excreting anything that may be unpleasant? It is simply harder to keep clean if you are filling your body with toxins.

Further reading:
"Comfort, Cleanliness and Convenience" - Elizabeth Shove
"Dress for Success" - John T. Molloy
"Style Bible" - Lauren Rothman
"Good Germs, Bad Germs" - Jessica Snyder Sachs

C - Perception

How do you see yourself? Do you think that it is more positive or more negative than reality? Why? It's good to see yourself as successful and as full of potential that your mind will allow and then a little more. You don't need the inflated ego that sometimes comes with knowing how good you are or can be. It's even worse to have the ego before you've accomplished anything. The superman is above ego and selfishness. Selfishness and ego feed each other. The more selfish you are the more highly you think of yourself and the more highly you think of yourself the more selfish you are. Have you met anyone that cares more about themselves than you? How long were they a part of your life? Why? Hopefully you don't even remember the last person that didn't listen to anything you had to say. You probably found them boring and inattentive. The reason a lot of us do remember them is because they rubbed us the wrong way by only thinking about themselves. They might have the highest opinion of you (you did listen to them after all), but you're always going to be beneath them in their eyes. At least that's how they make you feel. Some people don't even know they are doing it. They just talk and talk about themselves and their lives and you want to tell them to stop in a way that doesn't hurt their feelings.

Supermen don't want anyone to feel something they wouldn't want to feel. Especially that they are not important. A superman knows the importance of being a superman but with it comes the responsibility of knowing you are here to make everyone else in the world feel special too. Even if you are the king it can still hurt when people tell you that you are not the king. Until you get past the relation that has been created, the best you can feel about yourself comes from making others feel good. Looking in the mirror and saying wow, I sure am great may make you feel good but isn't it even better when someone else gives you a compliment? Of course it is. It makes you feel all warm and tingly inside like you are special. Even as supermen there is some part of us that likes to hear it though we don't crave it the way most people do. We can control everything we say and do but nothing that anyone else does. It's one of the hardest things about life and a lesson that is learned every day.

How you see yourself is important. The first person I asked, how do you see yourself told me, "With a mirror." Now he was a realist. You want to have the best possible self-image that you can without losing who you really are and your role as a superman. Never forget that you are here to help others recognize their potential and to bring everyone up to our level so that we may all live better. It's lonely at the top. Especially when you can't trust anyone because they're all trying to steal your throne. Wouldn't you rather help others up on to your level and have their support? Once there are enough people on top with you, they're going to start climbing higher and creating new heights for you to live up to with them. It only gets better with help from the right people. Your goal is to create the right people. It is an endless cycle that will keep us going higher and higher.

Perception is important to a superman. Perception of the self and perception of others shapes our lives more than we realize. For some people perception shapes their whole life. What they see they think is all real, no question. Seeing others as better or worse than you often leads to obstacles in life. It leads you to create the other person instead of letting the other person be who they are. The same goes for you. People you give potential will live up to more of it than you thought they could if you give them support and encouragement. Once we have created who another person is, it is hard for that person to grow out of our perception. The most successful people could end up being the least productive if we don't see all that they are capable of and more. The superman recognizes negativity in others as well as himself in order to help change it and never to make someone feel bad. Just the same, the superman doesn't give up just because someone else seems more capable.

One problem with perception is that we make everything personal. This person is like this toward me because of blank, I am this and I am not this, he or she does or doesn't like me. It's a guessing game that we give all of our faith. The truth is it doesn't matter. Any part of it may be true but so what? Does that have to make you feel good or bad any time you think of that person or yourself? Of course not! Be who you are and let them be who they are. They are either gaining success from it or losing success from it. You are instead getting ahead because of your objectivity and continued effort, not because someone else is trying to help you or hold you back. You are the superman, nothing can hold you back. Especially not others. Only yourself. Sound familiar? The only real thing in life that determines your success is you. Nothing else. Life is all about balance and outlook.

Let's get back to the beginning of this, how do you see yourself? Why not see yourself as infinitely capable? You are not invincible; you are just the person that can solve any problem the fastest and to the best possible outcome. You are someone who thinks before acting and does the best first because of that planning. Why not be the greatest? Wouldn't you like to live in a world of the greatest people instead of people who never think about what they could accomplish if they tried? Having everyone else try their best unlocks further potential in you. Their success gives you opportunities you never knew could exist. Make your self-image the best it can be. This doesn't mean ignore your faults. This is not an escape route. You don't look at yourself in the mirror and know you need to lose weight but say you are perfect the way you are. You look at yourself and say, "I'm losing weight," and then you do it. We don't accept things we can change about ourselves, we change them. It's as simple as that. You are the only one holding you back. Your attitude and the programming that you've heard your whole life.

If you don't think you can improve yourself you should have stopped reading this after the introduction. I doubt anyone unwilling to change would have picked up this book in the first place. Make the change. Be your ideal self instead of your perceived self. See it, hear it, believe it, live it. Freud defined these parts of us that so many people discredit or deny. They are simplified explanations for who we are but why did we ridicule this instead of taking it to heart and creating an ideal self? It was easier to be the id and have an excuse. Most people use explanations as excuses, they say, "see? This is that so I can't accomplish something" or "This is why it can't be done." That is incredible laziness that people don't even notice. Excuses. Take the truth and use it to better yourself, not as a reason why you can't or shouldn't. These are all things to look for in your day-to-day life.

Assignment: Real Versus Ideal

Your assignment is to think of your perceived self and your ideal self. Make two lists, one for each self. Now see what you can do to move from the first list to the second list. The superman is always perceived as the ideal self and will live up to it. If you already are your ideal self, read through this book and find things you can add to it or rewrite your list to make sure that you have everything where you need it. This list should surprise you at times when you realize what you are seeing is not really what you want to see. Always keep improving. Always. Be the superman not the everyman.

D - Light

Make sure you live with proper lighting... glow of a computer monitor is not the path to success or good health. Get enough sunlight! Doctors are recommending sunlamps for people that aren't getting outside often enough. This isn't just so you can have a nice tan and look socially pleasing, it's because the sun keeps you healthier. The sun provides us with Vitamin D and a sunny disposition. Seriously, people in sunnier states are generally happier people. I moved to a sunny state and everybody is friendly as can be. What's more, any time it starts raining everyone looks outside and starts smiling. How is that for having the right attitude? It could rain for two years straight and the people here would still smile and feel blessed. Not all of us have the luxury of living in the desert but you can still have the same attitude toward rain or shine.

As well, you should always wear sunscreen if you are going to be in the sun. Sunscreen helps prevent ultraviolet radiation from reaching the skin. The sun's rays can be harmful but you can use that to your advantage. Sunlight kills bacteria. Any man might notice that sometimes after a long nights rest the room doesn't smell that pleasant. Well, the fastest way to get rid of that smell is to open up the curtains and let the sunshine in! Bacteria thrive in environments with a lot of warmth, humidity and darkness. Let the sunlight in! There have been developments in lamp technology as well that have allowed the more helpful rays to reach people. If you don't have time to get out in the sun with your sunscreen on, buy a SAD sun lamp that will help improve your mood and provide Vitamin D. On top of everything it will help you start conversations with other people. They will want to know what it is and you can explain all the benefits of it, how you read about it in this book and how you are in charge of yourself and your life. Show them how good it feels and tell them they can be part of it too. In fact, tell them they already are part of it. It's just what they can do to cultivate it that has not become habit.

There are benefits to wearing sunscreen; I know a lot of people don't want to believe it. It will keep you looking young and will keep your skin healthier. I can't believe the amount of people that find reasons not to wear sunscreen. Whether they think they'll tan better or various other reasons they come up with, none of it is accurate. Wearing sunscreen will reduce your risks of sunburn, skin cancer, and protect you from the aging effects of the sun. You will notice that makeup has sunscreen in it as well; there is a reason for this. The sun is not good for your unprotected skin. Take care of your body and your skin, which is the biggest organ you have. It covers your whole body. I like to wear sunscreen because it makes me feel like I'm on vacation. I live in one of the sunniest places in America so I sure need it. When I'm at work, sometimes I'll smell it and remember the times I used to be on vacation and I'll feel happier because of it. Make everything you do enjoyable. If you can't find a way, you're not trying hard enough.

E - Eat at Home for Your Health

Create as many meals at home as you can. I don't even have to mention fast food and how horrible these things are that we put in our bodies. I don't think a lot of it is food. Cavemen didn't go hunting for a chicken nugget they went hunting for fresh organic food! It's a big craze and the reason is simple: they are showing you how to improve yourself and that healthy and organic foods will improve yourself, your health, your mind, and the lives of all of those animals. There is a difference between eating fresh healthy food and eating whatever they put in front of you. Eating what you purchase at the store and make at home is many times healthier than anything else that you can buy that is already prepared. This even includes frozen and canned foods that may be high in salt or sugar. Buy fresh fruits and vegetables as well as fresh produce and fresh meats. Cut back on fats. No more bacon, a lot less butter and cheese. Balance your diet and leave nothing out. On top of that control your portion size. Many thousands of pounds a year could have been kept off of everyday patriots if they decided not to overeat. Do you think restaurants are encouraging you to eat less? Of course not.

It's also good to take a vitamin in the morning. I know people say the results are inconclusive but I have to say any day I miss my vitamin, I feel sluggish and my appetite is more than doubled which I attribute to my body trying to get all of the extra substances that it didn't get when I missed my vitamin that morning. If you can keep on a healthy eating schedule without a vitamin that's fine too. Do whatever is healthiest and works for you. If it's not working give the vitamin a shot. That little vitamin isn't going to kill you or everyone buying them would be dead by now and they wouldn't have anyone to sell to. If you have tried a multivitamin and didn't like it, try a different one. Different people need different things in their diet and sometimes one that works for everyone won't be specific enough for you. When I first started taking vitamins my stomach would hurt every day. After years of pulling myself through the pain, my roommate in college told me to switch brands because he had the same problem. I listened to him and have felt great every day since and still have been able to take a vitamin in the morning.

The reason I say stay away from eating out is mainly so you can keep a balanced and healthy diet. There are very few places that will truly give you a healthy meal whether it's butter, fat and salt they load their food up with for taste, or portion size and encouraging bad habits such as drinking and eating a large dessert after you've had your fill. Resist the temptation to eat out and if you do, make a conscious effort to do it healthily. There are plenty of other books on how to eat properly and there are some on how to order healthy food in a restaurant. I hear it's keeping carbs away from meats. Fruit, vegetables and either meat or carbs is the way to go according to Brian Tracy. Don't mix meat and carbs. All of them play a part in your diet and knowing when to eat what is a big factor in living and having enough energy.

I don't want it to become a big factor, but there is an issue of money as well. It costs more to eat out than to go shopping and eat a healthy meal at home. You can eat luxuriously at half the price if you pay attention to prices. Products often go on sale, which gives you a good opportunity to try new things. That is the real reason things go on sale, so you'll try their product! You can even buy things you like when they're on sale and save money. Don't buy things you don't want or don't need just because they're on sale. Keep what you're buying specific to what will be healthiest for you.

Further reading:
"Dining Lean" - Joanne V. Lichten
"Eat Out, Eat Right" - Hope S. Warshaw
"Eat, Drink, and Be Healthy" - Walter Willett and P.J. Skerrett
"70 Healthy Habits" - S. J. Scott

One last thing on being physically healthy is to stay that way. Any time you think that something is not right, whether that pain in your foot has been there for too long or that sharp pain when you breathe might not be normal, schedule an appointment with your doctor to have it checked out. Preventative maintenance ends up being the cheaper alternative to what can happen if a problem is not discovered in time. Especially if it's one of the horrible things that you hear about on the news every night. People are fine one day and dead the next because they didn't tell anyone about a dull ache that they've had for months. A lot of things are not preventable but the ones that are can kill you if you aren't responsible. That being said, make sure to get your annual checkup from your doctor, your dentist, and maybe your psychiatrist.

Chapter 3 - Socially

A - Choosing the Right Company

The superman lives with other supermen. Make sure those around you are supermen as well. You are only as good as the company you keep. Make sure it's the best possible company. Fellow supermen. You can meet other supermen and help your friends to become supermen as well. It's easy to see who is going places in life and who is not. If you have to question whether it's someone you should be around or something you should be doing, it's probably not. With people you can say to them, "Hey, let's do something to improve ourselves" and give them a few ideas. If they don't like any of the ideas they're not someone you should be around. Before you do anything ask yourself how is this improving me in any of the categories? You have to have at least one good answer before you should commit to the activity. Just wanting to do it is not a good enough reason. What is it going to do for you? Don't forget that someone is willing to pay you for your time. You should be willing to pay yourself for your time and what you do when you're not at work. When it comes down to it you will either end up paying or being rewarded for everything in life.

B - Breaking Free

Part of being the superman is breaking the bounds of society. This is not breaking the law but breaking unspoken agreements that seem to hold us in place with everyone else. It's a slight of the hand that makes people question why everything is laid out the way it is; it gives people a taste of what they are missing, that little extra in life that you can do outside of what everyone and everything tells you is allowed. These activities give you a taste of life because once you stop following the same norms that everyone thinks they have to, you will live as a higher being. Things like asking your waiter to choose your entire meal for you. These little things are creative and fun but how many people will ever give up control like that or break the unspoken rule that you must choose what you're eating at a restaurant? Supermen break these boundaries all the time. Other people need these challenges to be reminded that they are not just machines. I am not suggesting that you break the law because you will face negative consequences for that. Instead, think about all of the rules that aren't even rules that people follow. Talk to your server at restaurants, ask what they are doing in life and who they want to become? Connect with human beings who are inside and outside of what you consider your social class because if you're stuck in your class, then to put it simply you're an imbecile. It's all part of our imaginations that we have power. Especially power over other people based on materialism. Talk to your mailman, policemen, everyone you normally nod to and stay away from. These workers will be a lot happier helping real people like them instead of empty faces. Bring humanity back into the workforce. Help people understand they are people and not drones. Wouldn't you like to know who you are helping by working all the time?

C - No One to Blame

Forget about blame. Blame holds us back. The time people spend worrying about what or who to blame perplexes me. They could have solved the problem five times over in the time they were being negative and eventually attacking someone else. It's not a good feeling for anyone involved. Drop blame out of your life. If you are surrounded by supermen you will see them take the opportunity to learn from the issue and overcome it. Normal people stew over problems and look worried and guilty, then eventually someone will attack someone else to try to shift this blame that has been created. This creates even more negativity and the opportunity for hurting others. Be the superman in every situation. It's not what has happened that we should be worrying about but how we are going to make it better. Don't carry problems, carry solutions. The human mind has been shaped this way by society, that we all need to worry, be negative and feel hopeless. In my world people aren't afraid to take credit for anything good or bad. This is because it's not blame and it won't hurt anyone's feelings; it will only help the situation. We learn from it and we help others to prevent it from happening to them. We should live in a world of positive encouragement that focuses on making things better instead of wasting time trying to find someone to hurt with blame and accusation.

D - Social Influences

People like to do what others around them are doing. People like to fit in and feel like they are a part of something. They create their world believing that everyone else in it will help them affirm its existence. They want to be liked and how do you make someone like you? By being like them. The super-mentality spreads itself simply by practice. The more people you are around the more people will be like you and the more it will spread. It will be seen as a weakness not to want to improve. It should be, it is a weakness! We shouldn't live our lives valuing laziness, yet so many people do just that without even knowing it. I mentioned earlier that you should surround yourself with supermen, this is not just for your benefit but for their benefit as well. If you are around people that practice like activities, they are going to be much more likely to practice them as well, just as you are more likely to practice whatever they are doing. If you cannot overcome the need to fit in, join your fellow superman where you will fit in and improve yourself in the process.

E - Keeping a Positive Attitude

We should be as pleasant as we can to everyone else in the world. As I mentioned earlier most people are not ready to see the world the same way we do. They are comfortable and out of fear they will fight change and even improvement. They will complain about everything and never take the first step. We need to behave in polite society in order to help keep the people that are stuck in higher spirits. They will never break out from negativity through this social nicety, only through love and understanding. They don't realize that we're trying to help them through our efforts, and their attachment to what they think we're taking away is misguided. They think they will feel loss for the life they are living when most of them aren't even happy with that life. They put value on all the wrong things and end up with nothing when they die. So do your best to keep them in a positive mindset just like you would want others to do for you. Try to cheer people up and do nice things for them. Acknowledge everybody you pass as they are part of humanity just like you and me, even if they don't realize it. This is the message that every spiritual leader has been trying to teach for thousands of years. All the way back to the first rule ever created, treat others like you want to be treated. Do unto others as you would have others do unto you. The golden rule. It's the first thing we teach our children and yet at our age we have lost it completely. Take it to heart and feel your love for everybody and make sure to let them feel it as well so the world can be a better, safer place for all of us. One thing we need to realize about it is that the rule doesn't state that we should do unto others as we have done unto ourselves, but that we should do unto others as we **want and would prefer to have** done unto ourselves. This means there will be times when things that happen to us are not as we would do unto others, but that does not grant us permission to do the same to someone else.

F - Gifts and Love

Love is the best thing to have in your life. Cultivate it wherever possible. Don't accept anything less than love from yourself and from others at everything you do. Share and spread love by doing things for those less fortunate and even those more fortunate if you are able. Fortunate can be a funny thing. You may think someone is happy because you would be in their situation, but they may not feel the same way. Share love by surprising others and being thoughtful in any way possible, from taking out the garbage to buying them flowers or something that they've been wanting.

Do not bestow unto the superman material goods as he has little need for them. It goes against our ideal to be materialistic and have attachment for that which helps neither us nor anyone else. Supermen are happy just to have you around and if you insist upon buying a gift, make sure it is something they can use to live or improve themselves. Food that you have made yourself is a great offering because you are giving the time it took you to make it, and it is something that you have created. Most people go through their lives without creating anything. Gift giving is harder with other supermen because they don't place the same value in material goods but they will be just as happy as anyone else if you get them that book on self-improvement they've been wanting or simply compliment them as they should with you as well. Supermen appreciate the sincerity of a gift regardless of the value of that gift. We are thankful and we are happy to do things for other people in expectation of more love for the whole world, not anything directly given back to us.

The superman lives by the golden rule that we teach our kids but rarely practice. If you would want someone to do something for you, do it for them as well. Keep want out of it. The minute you do something because you expect something in return is the minute you find yourself with nothing. **The superman does not want or expect anything from anybody but himself.** Everything additional is considered more love in the world, not something the superman deserves from others. The supermen recognize that want and deserving is man made. It was created along with materialism to spread negativity and to keep people preoccupied in their imagined world. The superman has nothing in life that was not earned by the actions the superman has lived and performed. The love received from others is accepted warmly and graciously and is thought of as a direct result for all of the love that the superman has, does, and is going to put out there for the rest of the world to benefit from. As supermen we are more interested in creating a better world than just about improving our own world. The truth is the world and our world will become better by improving everything we can and will not become better through selfishness.

Chapter 4 - Spiritually

A - Who is this God Fellow Anyway?

What if people say we think we are Gods. Every religion I have studied has made us Gods, why should we not think that way? Christians believe that God is inside of us, we are created in his image, God is everything. Isn't that saying that not only is God a part of us, but that we are part of God? We must realize the God in all of us and live through His will and His power that is a part of everything. God has given us himself and not letting it out is what keeps people from being the superman. The Tao, Zen, Buddhism, etc... they all believe that everything is one, we are all one, part of everything. We have all of existence inside of us and we don't know how to control it, let it out, and realize the superman within. Our whole lives we are programmed to hold ourselves back. We are taught that we can only do and accomplish so much. We are given negativity and we use it as a reason we cannot excel or rise above what everyone else says we can. You must realize there is nothing holding us back and the walls that have been created in your mind do not exist.

B - The Beauty of Religion

Religion is such a controversial topic, people have killed over it, which doesn't sound like anything religion is supposed to be teaching us, but here it is dividing people.

I specialize in what you need to hear and what will make a difference. My aim is to show the things religion can offer that are hard to find in everyday life. Things like faith, hope, personal strength, guidance, motivation, peace, relaxation, habit, connection with others personally and socially, and something to overlook in polite conversation. If that doesn't sell you on it I don't know what will.

Religion motivates us. Everybody wants to be a part of something. Throughout history so much has been done in the name of God and what people interpreted from His messages. I never said they were right. We may never know if they were or not but look at all they've done. Look at the empires built by religion. Look at all of the people who are loving parents because that's what their religion said they should do. Look at all of the people who stay out of prison for following the rules we were taught as children by our religion. We may not have listened to them if they were clearly man made. Look at all of the people who turn their lives around after they have a religious experience. I'm sure you know someone like that. Why does it matter if the message is the same one you believe or not if it provides so much good in the world? Once you see right and wrong as perception, you will no longer worry what other people think and do.

A lot of people look toward religion as something they have to believe in. If it helps you, yes you should believe in it. You have the choice when it comes to religion. Nobody else should decide for you what you believe and what you use of it to benefit the world. When it comes down to it, religion is a tool. It is there to help us get past grieving, fear of death and fear in general. Religion is a conscious choice for the superman. Belief is personal to all of us and should be kept that way. The more belief one has the stronger they can use this religion in their lives, but even a little will go a long way. Find something, anything, to believe in and give it a chance.

C - The Power of Prayer

Prayer is very powerful. Even if you believe nothing will come of it, you can still have the same rewards from it. It gives us peace of mind and the feeling that we did all we could when we felt helpless. It gives us hope. It shapes change in your mind (remember what you put in will come back out). If you think about something you want constantly the world helps provide it to you. At the end of the day, prayer gives you a routine that you can follow. Little habits help keep our mind at peace and prevent anxiety. You show me a person who doesn't like habits and I'll show you a dirty, malnourished, unemployed, sleep deprived man with nothing to accomplish in life. That's because he doesn't shower regularly, brush his teeth, go to bed on time, get up on time, go to work every day or set goals for himself. Habit, when used correctly, can help bring order to our lives. I have already mentioned habits, goals and change throughout this book because of how powerful these things are.

At the end of the day, religion has more to offer in benefits when believed in and applied correctly. Like every good thing it can be misused and cause damage to our society, but there would be no hope left for any of us if we had nothing to believe in. I urge you strongly to carry out the next assignment if you want to add something to your life that will be of great benefit. **It does not matter what is real and what is unreal, it is what we take from it and how we use it that matters.**

Assignment: Find Your Beliefs and Gain Strength Through Them

Look into yourself and think about what you believe in. If you are already associated with a religion use it to it's fullest. Participate in events, pray every day and give yourself something that can empower you every day in your thoughts and in your life. If you don't have anything religious in your life, consider the options. Take a look at all of the religions there are in the world and find one that seems like it has enough merit for you to be a part of it. If you are an atheist you won't have quite as many benefits as other people do, but you can still look for solace in the peaceful absence of an afterlife and the thought that you are the only one in control of your life. This means you are responsible and can change anything you want. If you absolutely must believe in nothing, find a local group of atheists, if there is one, and join it so you can at least participate in community events with like-minded people. Try on a few religions if you need to. You may never find the right one if you don't try more than one. Practice a different religion every week and consult with leaders of that religion until you find a groove that is right for you. It doesn't even have to be an organized religion. You can worship in your own way and still reap similar benefits. You can take consolation in an afterlife, believe that there is someone helping you along the way in life, pray, celebrate, and think just as deeply about your beliefs as anyone else can.

Further reading:
"Holy Bible: King James Version"
"Autobiography of a Yogi" - Paramahansa Yogananda
"My Way: The Way of the White Clouds" - Osho
"The Living Gita: The Complete Bhagavad Gita - A Commentary for Modern Readers" - Sri Swami Satchidananda
"World Religions" - John Bowker
"The Religions Book" - DK Publishing
"Religion for Atheists: A Non-Believer's Guide to the Uses of Religion" - Alain De Botton

Section VII - Relaxing and De-stressing

Chapter 1 - Negative Distraction

Knowing how and when to relax and de-stress is an important part of living a healthy life. Positive vs. negative distraction. Know the difference between a positive and negative distraction so that you may avoid the negative ones. A positive distraction is love momentarily stopping you from completing a task. For example, when you are hard at work and your child comes into the office and wants a hug. If you love your family and your son this should be a moment for positive relaxation. Yes, your son is a distraction from your work, but he is being a positive distraction in that he only wants to take a little bit of your time to share love with you. You can take time out of any task you are working on for a positive distraction, but don't forget that positive distractions are still distractions and they should not take so much time as to become negative distractions. They should only occur once in a while because they do distract you from completing a task; too much of any kind of distraction is not a good thing whether it is a positive or negative distraction.

Relaxation is one of the best ways to de-stress and when you get back to work you will be that much more refreshed and ready to accomplish the task at hand. Relaxing does not have to be a distraction; it can be a realization of everything. You want to realize your own existence and feel how you fit into this world and are a part of everything. The knowledge that you are the most powerful of all beings and that at this moment you are able to take time to appreciate simply existing. Most people get into this state without even knowing it. For example, when you are playing golf or exercising. It puts you into a zone and helps your body relax even if it is a strenuous activity. It may be as easy as sitting down and feeling bliss in nothingness or it may require one of the methods of improvement to relax. The best relaxations are considered improvement. Reading a book, hiking, exercising, yoga, meditation, getting a massage, and even eating can all be relaxing. Anything you do consciously with a silent mind. Another good way of relaxing is tuning yourself with nature.

Go somewhere uninterrupted by humanity. There will be no technology, just you and the world and what it was before we adjusted it. There is only one thing that can be "relaxing" but does not improve you. That is negative distractions.

Negative distractions are anything in your life that does the opposite of improvement. It is what we consider giving in. Everything that stops us from being present and reaching our goals. Things your brain tells you that it wants when it is far from necessary. Staying on a computer for ten hours makes you feel numb, it doesn't make you feel good. Most negative distractions are a form of escapism. The urge to get away through things that distract us instead of things that help us overcome. These are usually time wasters that accomplish nothing beside the use of your time. Here are the obvious ones: alcohol, smoking, drugs, television, video games, computer use. **If it is not helping you improve, it is holding you back.**

Remember the people who didn't want to do anything with you to improve themselves? These are the things that they are likely doing. The temporary gratification that they receive from escapism and distractions is fake and it leaves as fast as it came. This addiction that people have to unimportant things in their life that they are using as a drug has to stop in order for us to progress. As supermen we start by understanding which distractions are positive and which are negative and removing the negative from our lives and replacing them with positive. Once you break free of the drug like addiction that negative distractions have upon your life, you feel a weight lifted. You feel free. There is no boredom for the superman because the superman knows how much there is to do all the time. There is no need for time wasters anymore, just real life.

Assignment: Realizing Distraction

Get that notebook out again if for some reason you put it away. Even when you're not reading it should be within your grasp. This time make a new list of things that distract you throughout your day. Once the list is completed mark which ones are positive and which ones are negative. Take the negative ones and find ways you can eliminate them from your life. It may be easy and it may be hard but once you eliminate that distraction (the harder it is, the more rewarding) you will find yourself free. There may be a feeling of discouragement the first few weeks of not getting your fix of negative distractions but fight against it until you are truly free. You will be surprised at how much more productive you are and how much happier your life will become. Just like everything else, you have to believe it and fight to make it a reality. Once you do, you will be flying above the clouds. The hardest part of fighting gravity is the initial propulsion to get us off of the earth and out of the atmosphere. From there the slightest push will keep us on a course indefinitely.

Chapter 2 - Why Relax?

We do need to relax in life because running anything at full speed for too long will cause it to break down. The machine that we are needs to relax just like any other machine. It is a process of relaxing and thereby de-stressing. You can work optimally under less pressure.

Before we can work at minimizing stress we must first take a look at the different kinds of stress. What are some things that make you feel stress? The two largest categories for stress are lasting and temporary stress. Lasting stress is the kind that builds up inside of you for years, pushing and pulling and tugging away at you until you die years before your time. It is the kind of stress that gives you a heart attack through degraded health and lets you get sick easier because your immune system is working too hard. It is the kind of stress that makes you pull out your hair or bite at your nails. Lasting stress comes from anything that stresses you that you do repeatedly throughout your life. Letting your full time job be frustrating or letting yourself get mad all the time. These are things that build over time and will always lead you to a life or death moment when the doctor tells you it's time to either stop participating or stop living. We don't have to wait until that time to open our eyes. Don't let things make you angry! Don't let things make you feel pressured. You are going to work your hardest and try your best and if it doesn't work out, the world has a different plan for you.

Who we have been programmed to be thinks that all of this matters and it takes stress from its perception of pressure. Never fear the consequences that are being put upon you because that fear is usually a thousand times more damaging than the actual outcome. People and corporations who want more from you are the ones who use fear against you so they can control you. They want you to do more for less at your own expense. They do unethical things like firing other people and giving you their work to do at the same salary you already earn. Never trust people who want to give you more without recompense. It is up to you to decide how much more you do, not them. They will continue to take if you let them. Find a better job where you will be rewarded for working harder, not expected to do it for free. Supermen do not let other people take advantage of them. We give freely of our own hearts, but in time we see who will give back and who will continue taking. Then we will stay around the people who give and leave the people who take.

Temporary stress is a form of stress that we can easily recover from. Stress that comes with things like staying awake too long. They are easily fixed and in some cases you can simply go to sleep! Something as simple as sleeping the right amount of time every night or eating breakfast can make all the difference. These little stressors are small but they can be frequent as well and may be impairing your day-to-day life without you even knowing it. The usual reaction to temporary stress is also temporary. Some people dwell on it. It can last longer and become lasting stress, but it starts out temporary and should stay that way.

Our goal is to eliminate lasting stress and to keep temporary stress low enough to be healthy but also motivating. Experiencing stress is part of everyday life and there is an optimal level of stress that you should live by. Cutting it out altogether can be a new stage of enlightenment but most often it leads to unproductivity in your own self-improvement. Stress keeps you alert and is helpful in reaching deadlines in some situations. In others, holding on to stress will kill you. If someone was selling stress in a box there would be the same Surgeon General's warning on the box as there is on cigarettes. Stress has been known to cause heart failure and premature death. You can help yourself to live longer by following a healthy lifestyle. If you are following this book you should not have that much to worry about anymore. Once you have the proper mental, physical, social and spiritual diet you will have eliminated most of the stress from your life. Keep track of your blood pressure; if it is higher one day ask yourself why, because that is a stressor in your life and you need to take control of it. Go to your doctors regularly to make sure your health is on track as well. They will be among the first to tell you to relax.

Assignment: Working Through Stress

Nobody said that becoming the superman would be easy. It is not something you can achieve by sitting on your couch or putting in a half-hearted effort. You have gotten this far so I know you are determined to improve yourself and live a longer, happier, better life. Go to the next page in your notebook and write down everything you can think of that stresses you out. Once the list is made write down the worst thing that could happen in each situation. You'll notice that none of them is really that bad. Again, your perception of how bad things are comes from your programming, not truth. Imagine yourself a year from now after the worst from that event has happened. What then? Are you going to still be able to live your life and improve? Naturally you are. You're going to read this book and have the right attitude and mindset to achieve success in every situation, whether it works out how it was planned or even better.

These little things that stress us out are inconsequential when you look at life as a whole and what we should really be accomplishing on this earth. When you find yourself feeling stressed out think about how bad it will be at it's worst, you create the opportunity for the worst to happen and bring it into the now. The worst thing that can happen is exactly what is stopping everybody else, it is the fear that comes with the unknown and change. When it comes down to it, stress is caused by fear. You are scared of what will happen instead of embracing uncertainty and knowing that you will be able to make your life however you want to make it, no matter what happens.

Now make a list of all the stress you still can't get out of your life but before each item write, "I no longer feel stress because of," and every day read this list aloud to yourself when you wake up and before you go to bed. This is to help program your brain into what you already know to be true. You don't need to feel stress the way you do with these things and after a few weeks of saying it, it will come to be.

Chapter 3 - Take Breaks

Take time for breaks. Even the great painter/creator Leonardo Da Vinci took breaks while he was working. You can't stay in the zone for too long without a break. You will be most productive like Da Vinci if you work for a certain amount of time then take a short break to re-energize yourself. The greatest minds of our time knew that taking a break would allow us to work with a higher degree of accuracy and success. It is the simple idea of a cool down period. You can even do this by switching to a different task for a short time and coming back to the other one later. Like everything in the world, we start to stagnate when we do one thing for too long. Even things that benefit us. We start to do things less efficiently if we do them for too long. That is why we don't put our entire workweek into the two days; imagine the energy it would take if we did it all at once.

When you start to feel drained or feel as though you have hit a roadblock or are even just working a little less efficiently than you want to, take a break and reinvigorate yourself. There wouldn't be laws about providing breaks to employees if it weren't beneficial. You will need to take your breaks responsibly. Don't take a break every few minutes. Work at least an hour for every ten-minute break you take and as often as possible use that time to do something else productive and useful, just of a different nature. Say you are driving down the road and you notice by the temperature gauge that your car is overheating. You don't keep driving down the road unless you want to damage the car. You pull over and wait a bit to let the car cool down before continuing on your journey. In that time, instead of just letting the car sit there, you can clean it out, wash the windows or check the air pressure in your tires. These are all useful things that will stimulate your brain and body differently than driving. Instead of just letting the car rest, you are helping to keep it in top condition. Just like yourself. You are not just resting for the rest and the break time, you are resting so you will be able to perform better and at the same time maintain yourself and improve yourself any way that you can.

Although the superman is dedicated to improvement, the superman understands that there is a time to relax and reenergize throughout the day. The superman is afraid of being idle but knows not to overwork himself in a way that could be harmful. Even God took a day to rest. This is where balance comes in. Balancing out the areas of improvement prevent stagnation and overworking. Even if it were possible to focus on one constantly, it would not be a well-rounded or balanced form of self-improvement and shows lack of self-control. It goes back to doing what is easiest instead of what is best. In the main areas of improvement, some of them will be easier than others. We must make sure to have a schedule and goals for this reason. Evaluate your skill level in each area and adjust your schedule and how you perform each mission accordingly. You should focus most on the ones you want to do the least because it is likely that those are areas in your life that need the most improvement.

Chapter 4 - How do You Change Anything in Life?

People come to me and say, "I have too much stress in my life but I can't change it, I have to stay at a job I hate with people that get me down." It is a challenge to point out all of the things wrong with that sentence. "I can't" is not a phrase you will ever hear from the superman. "I have to" when referring to anything you don't like is on the same list. "People get me down" is putting the blame on others, giving away the control, and creating blame. These are people that need the message we are teaching. Back to the original excuse: they are unhappy with their job because it stresses them out too much but feel it is the only way they can continue financially supporting themselves and their family. There are many things I can tell you to fix this. It would be easiest to turn these statements around and start to love your job through self-talk and positive attitude! The biggest thing you might have to do is to find a new job! Beyond that, what is the big deal? It's only because you think it's hard that it really is hard. It's simple if you make the effort to change.

You are the only one who knows what you love to do and you must learn to profit from doing what you love, instead of what you feel you are forced to do. You can find that by talking to others, and sharing your interest. You don't have to leap into it. Start with a hobby in your spare time and spend everything you can on improving your knowledge on the subject and finding a way to profit from it short term. The best way, as I mentioned, is to change how you feel. Make the same two lists about your job, good and bad. Turn the bad into good and read it every time you have a negative thought regarding anything about your job. If you can find ways to initiate positive changes instead of just complaining, that's even better and you will be seen as innovative and as a leader. Supermen are leaders.

Find goals for your job, even if it is to enjoy your time at work; think of everything that is stopping you and turn those things into strengths or even better, change them. I know that you're thinking you can't change things and that no one listens to you. That's because of your attitude! With the right attitude you can change things, it's a positive attitude that brings solutions to people instead of problems. Things are only set in their tracks when you stop trying to push them in the right direction. It's easy when you are the superman. Did one person turn down your idea? Tell another person. Ask how it can be a better idea. Make it their idea. As long as it is accomplished and makes your life better you are on your way to loving your job. If the idea needs more work and thought, put more work and thought into the idea then bring it back to the table. The main reason people turn down ideas is because they are unsure and need more convincing. The other reason is that they don't want to be the one to do any work for it. Take responsibility for your idea and put the action on you, not on other people. If you don't want to eventually move on from this job to do what you really love, then make your goal to love the job you have.

Always do your best at the job you have in order to get the job you want. There is no need to limit yourself. You may want to find another job that starts in a position where you can advance or you may already be in one, but don't ever think that you have to be where you are instead of where you want to be. Do you want a promotion? Make it happen. People that move up in the world are never compensated for how much more they do right away. They are always doing more to get further because they can see the bigger picture. If we were only compensated for what we did, we would already be working harder than we do. You have to realize that the compensation for your extra work now is promotion, future recognition and the satisfaction that is a result of the extra work you have already accomplished above the work you were expected to do. It is not just working hard, doing more, and accomplishing more (though those are a big part of it), the biggest part of moving up is with a positive attitude and hard work. You will have to give a lot to other people to move up in many jobs. Make them look good, make them feel good, make them important. That can come from the work you do but it also comes from the way you interact with them.

The people above you need to see the benefit in having you up there with them instead of down below. This is hard a lot of the time because of unmotivated bosses that don't want to work harder so they keep you under them as long as possible to get more done. I don't blame them for wanting to keep you with them but they should know from the start that you're going to be there no matter what level you are on and that if you cannot advance, then you cannot continue working for them. Supermen are not afraid of competition. They are the ones that care about the business more than themselves as individuals. They will do what is best for the company at whatever cost is necessary. They are the ones happy to see successful people do well and they are the first to reward hard work and a positive attitude. They are not concerned with their own position in the company because they are working just as hard and know that both of you are just as valuable no matter where and what position they will be in.

Chapter 5 - Evaluate Your Stress

Think of what is stressing you out and why. Think of the worst possible outcome of what you are getting stressed out about and what you would do in that situation. First take a look at how realistic it is that that will happen. Most of the time it's a complete exaggeration and it will help you see the lighter side of things. Nothing that bad is going to happen. On top of that, it's unlikely that the worst thing that could happen will happen and if it does you're ready for it now, what is there to worry about?

As a child you may have been stressed out about having to learn how to tie your shoelaces. The worst thing that could happen is that your shoe would come untied and people would laugh at you (at least you believed this would happen when in reality your teacher or another adult would have helped you tie it and everyone else would understand because they felt just as nervous it would happen to them!). Remember, there is always something worse that can happen even if you think what you're worried about is bad.

On the flip side there is always something better. You shouldn't give time to worry instead of progress. Put it into perspective. If this one thing goes wrong in your whole life, so what? There is always somewhere to go from there, stop worrying so much about it. You can solve the problem twice in the time and energy you are using to worry. That energy is creating negativity in your life and anxiety. Listen to Dale Carnegie's "How to Stop Worrying" and take his advice to heart and I am completely convinced that your life will be easier and more fulfilling. Back to the shoe tying, after you did it over and over it became easy. Now do you worry about your shoe coming untied during the day? I hope not. If that were the biggest of your problems you wouldn't have a very challenging life would you? The same goes for what you are worrying about right now. If you dealt with it every day for a year it would be a piece of cake and one day it will be.

Assignment: Understand Your Stress

Think about everything that stresses you out in life. Decide that you want change and brainstorm ideas on paper of how you can change these things. It can be simple or complex, short term or long term. Write out all of the things that will help you deal with these and any other stressful situations. Once they are in front of you and you know you want change in your life...do it! It really is that simple. You'll feel better, live longer and generally be more fun to be around, believe me. Remember, you can only change if you believe you can. I have seen and had habits broken in my own life just by being convinced that they would be. At the beginning I wasn't all that convinced but I stuck to it and before I knew it I saw the change and was shocked that it had been so easy! The key is to notice it right away and tell yourself that it's not the way it is but the way you want it to be. Once you do that everything will work out just fine.

Section VIII - The Next Steps

Chapter 1 - Don't Give Up

You are not helpless to change no matter what you've been programmed to believe. Everyone that is willing to try and try again will always allow and embrace change. Those who give up and accept failure are helpless. The superman does not accept failure and sees anything that stands in the way as a test of willpower and strength. The superman is successful because of the amount of obstacles overcome, not because there was nothing standing in the way. One who gets by in a life without obstacles, didn't get by anything at all.

Chapter 2 - Never Stop Building (Stagnation)

To stop building and improving is considered stagnation. It is among the biggest enemies of the superman. It sneaks into our lives when we least suspect it, leading to the issues that plague the nation (laziness, greed, sloth, envy). It leads to a dependency on all but the self for everything in life. It should be one of the most feared of the issues we face in both day-to-day life and long term success. Keeping track of your life with a set schedule and goals will keep this issue at bay. It is when we take easier paths that are less rewarding that we end up in the grips of this enemy called stagnation.

Stagnation is a big issue because it can come from every angle. One day we are building ourselves up and later we end up stagnating by not raising our goals and by letting what once was a lot to us, become very little. In this regard it comes not only from lack of accomplishment, but lack of greater accomplishment. For example, when you can't run a mile, running a mile is a big deal to you and if you keep doing it, one day it will become easy for you. Now the question: Is it more of an accomplishment for you to run a mile now when it is easy or before when it seemed out of reach? The clear answer is it's more of an accomplishment to do something you can't do than it is to do something that comes with little difficulty. So, if you continued running a mile for the rest of your life it wouldn't be very much of an accomplishment because you reached that goal years ago. This is the stagnation that we are blinded to by the appearance that we are still accomplishing our goal. Running that mile may keep you in better shape and good health but you're stuck. Your improvement system in this area is stagnating.

This is why supermen need to be, and often are, promoted before anyone else. Most people do the bare minimum they have to do in order to get money. Money is actually the least important of the numerous rewards you get at work. The most important thing is the improvement you pay yourself for working harder and learning more every day. This in turn makes you worth more. Supermen get more out of themselves in everything that is accomplished and get more out of everyone and everything else in life. Even if you don't see the next step, keep improving yourself until you do. When it is clear to you what you need to do, you will already have almost reached the next goal that was there all along.

Stagnation is a mortal enemy in our everyday lives. It encourages us to do less and less and to expect more for nothing. All of these things that are invented to make our lives easier are actually making it harder for us to learn and improve. Most people don't even know how to change a tire anymore. Someone else can do that for you. There are times in your life when you may have people working for you. Not until then should you expect anyone else to do something for you and even then it is for the company more than it is for you. You should have employees to do the less important things at your job so that the things they cannot do that make you the most successful will fill your time completely. They say you should delegate any task that someone else can do at least 80 percent as well as you can. That is assuming that there is something important you do with that free time that no one else can do. You're not giving away work to lighten your load; you're giving away your work so that you can take on larger projects and bigger things that are within your reach. The superman does everything he can on his own as long as the most important things are being done efficiently. The superman takes the appropriate amount of time to relax and recharge. He then makes sure his goals are set high enough to improve and that stagnation is not taking hold of him.

Assignment: Getting Past Stagnation

Get out your notebook again and get ready to make a list. What in your life is stagnating? Is there an assignment you left half finished? Is there something you pay someone else to do when it would be beneficial for you to do it and learn from it? If it's something that would be a productive use of your time compared to what you are doing now, learn it. If there is something bigger you do, make sure the person that does your smaller tasks is happy and accomplishing as much as they can as well.

Are you accomplishing the same thing today you did last year or accomplishing more? The answer should be more. How often do you read? More or less than last year? Are you spending more time watching TV? Are you spending the right amount of time with your family? Are you working too hard or not hard enough? Are there time-consuming activities at work that someone else can do just as well? What is the learning in your life like? What is your improvement in all of the subjects in this book looking like about now? Write down all of it, every harsh and cruel detail and see all of the invisible demons that plague the world. Once you have your list all lined up, on the other side of the sheet answer what you can and should do to solve these issues of stagnation. Recognize these things any time you see them occur in your life. Now that you know what they are you can notice them taking up your time.

If you have to, take post-it notes and place them on everything that wastes your time so that you may be reminded even easier that you are wasting time. Put one on your television, one on your cigarettes, one on the background of your cell phone, one on your refrigerator. These may be things you do enjoy now, but that enjoyment will seem miniscule when you see how successful you really can be without them. What else can you do in the areas that you are already improving? More importantly, what can you do to eliminate the areas that have been stagnating for the longest? Use all of the answers you wrote down on what you can and should be doing and add it to the goals page you already made. Set time constraints on these goals as guidelines and then raise them again once they are met.

Chapter 3 - Attitude

A - Become the Superman

You don't have to move mountains. You are the superman, you can move mountains and your attitude should reflect that. This is not acting like you can but being confident that you can. There are always things beyond our control, but we shall not acknowledge anything as beyond our control lest we put it there through belief. We are the universe, we control everything, and if something happens in a way that we did not intend, it was meant to be and the superman shall build through this experience not get pulled down. Every roadblock provides us with something to strive to rise above. We are lucky to have challenges in our lives so that we may prove our worth and prove ourselves as supermen. It is often said that attitude is everything. Attitude is not everything, you just can't get anywhere good without the right one. Attitude is the stepping-stone onto the path of life. You could swim the whole way or you can see the rocks and walk across. Positive attitude takes us down a positive path. Negative attitude leaves us deserted. We've often heard that people will be chosen for a job based on their attitude over qualifications. This is the whole purpose of a job interview. If they just wanted to know what you can do, they would have read your resume and hired you based on qualifications alone. They perform the interview to make sure you have the right attitude. They won't employ the smartest man in the world if he has the wrong attitude, nor should they. I have already talked about negativity earlier and how it gets you nowhere. In this chapter I want to do the opposite. I want to show you the value of positivity.

B - A List of Positive Things

Exercising in moderation but on a schedule
Creating and following good habits
Listening to positive life changing audiobooks
Scheduling
Setting goals
Sincerely complimenting others
Reading
Giving recognition
Proper diet
Positive attitude
Spreading love to those in need
Trust
Relaxation
Moderation
Letting go
Being passionate
Exploring
Trying positive new things

I am sure you have other things to add to this list and feel free to do so. Make a similar list for yourself as a guideline when you are setting goals and making any of the lists this book mentions.

C - Be the Best

I want you to do better than me in life. I'm not going to make that easy for you but I want to see you rise even higher than I have and the most successful people in the world have because I know you have it in you, all of you. I know you can be at the top of the list of successful people and I am here to help you get there. I can only help you to see the path, you need to follow it. You are going to follow it. You are the superman. You are part of a select few who are thinking clearly. You see all that you are going to become and the limitless potential waiting for you to reach out and grab it. You are the greatest person you will ever know and by being here with me right now you are part of the most select group of people in the world that are going to be right there next to you pushing and pulling you to reach your full potential.

D - Fill Your Life with Love

Fill your life with positivity and things that make you happy and lead you to want to improve. Keep improvement and progress in the front of your mind. What do you love? Your family, perhaps a pet? Get pictures of who or what you love and put them everywhere. Put them all around your house, in your office, on your desktop background, on your dashboard. Keep the things you love within your vision so you can always feel their presence in your life. Whatever they cause you to feel will be reflected in your life if you keep them present.

What do you like to do? What are you passionate about? Find whatever that is and buy books about the subject. If you can get books and audiobooks or programs (languages especially) to help you learn more about the subject, do it! Buy at least ten different things you can use to study and appreciate the subject. If it is hard for you to pick up these books, you're not really passionate or you don't really care about one of the most important things in your life! This is one of the key fundamentals to mental improvement. It is easy to learn more about what you love and there are so many resources available. If you are dedicated to improvement, you will find countless books and topics that you like and add those to what you are reading and hearing about as well! Then you will find yourself excelling at your current job and everything you are doing as well as building your ability to perform exceedingly well at what you are passionate about.

Section IX - Make the Change

Chapter 1 - Inspiration, What is your Muse?

Inspiration leads us to keep trying and to reach the very limits of existence in order to accomplish our goals.

Are you inspired by a loved one or the cheese puffs on the kitchen counter that are waiting when you reach your goal? Either one can provide you with the same motivation even though the cheese puffs are going to be more fleeting. They will both need constant renewal. You can do this by replacing your muse, finding a new muse, or renewing the muse (most rewarding). Renewing the muse in the case of a loved one is easy and rewarding, you must cultivate your love for this person and what it is that ignites the divine spark between you two. Renewing the cheese puffs will take more time because you will have to make them from scratch. Buying new ones is not renewing it is replacing. The same goes for finding a new person in your life for motivation instead of cultivating the relationship you already have. It's unsatisfying and if you replace one time, you are more likely to continue replacing instead of keeping and cultivating what it is that drives your inspiration.

Find a muse! Whatever it is make sure your muse provides inspiration to continue whatever it is you are trying to achieve. For me it is the superman and being the superman. Through my journey to become the superman I realized that I was the superman and that anyone can be. Being a superman is my muse. I am inspired by the fact that I can be greater than human and help others to realize this as well. It provides you with motivation, determination and it is something to cheer you up when you think you don't have what it takes. Success and improvement are also my muse. What I want to be in the future is strong enough motivation for me to do what I need to do right now in order to get there.

A muse provides you with support, determination, drive, dedication, company (someone to talk to), and a renewed sense of vigor to continue the path toward reaching your goal!

Don't set your muse on a pedestal. Even if your muse is a fellow superman you must realize we are all fallible, especially those who have just begun their journey as supermen. The people we put the highest got there by climbing and falling and climbing and falling. Nobody gets to the top without falling a few times and the people we look up to are right along side the climbers. The supermen are ahead of most people as muses because they will be there right by your side the whole way as will anyone with the same goals as you. We look up to other superman and they look back with the same respect as brothers. If you idolize your muse, it is likely that they will let you down if you give them enough time. This is through no fault of their own but through your expectation. Expect them to fail just as often as you expect yourself to fail. This does not mean they aren't someone to look up to, it just means you need to help each other out through the difficult times.

Chapter 2 - Don't Hold Back

Don't let anything hold you back in life. Ever. The only difference between someone who is successful and someone who is not is that one of them did something about it and didn't give up until they were where they wanted to be. The superman does not give up, does not accept defeat and never stops improving. We may stray from our path from time to time but we must recognize these moments and grow from them. The path is not a straight one for most, but it does lead to the same place of success and satisfaction.

Chapter 3 - Do What You Love, Love What You Do

Do what you love and do what you're good at. Be good at what you love, kill two birds with one stone. Love what you do. Often times a love for what you do will be enough to make it something you enjoy. You won't always be in a position where you are able to do only what you love. No matter what you do in life do your best and keep a positive attitude. Enjoyment comes from within you, not always from your circumstance or what you are doing. You have to choose to enjoy and make the best of every situation. You are encouraged to do whatever will make you the happiest in life; but realistically nobody does only what they want to do 100 percent of the time and claims the happiness they thought they would gain from it. I do recommend that you find passion in your life not just for becoming the superman, but for living your life to the fullest. Sometimes you won't be able to do what you love until you succeed at something else and build a solid foundation in your life in order to provide stability for when you choose to take up doing what you love. Enjoy what you do all the time. There are plenty of ways to do that and once you follow proper procedures you can end up loving what you started off hating. A lot of people may need to follow such methods in order to convince themselves to become the superman. It doesn't matter how you become a superman; whether you start off as the superman or have to talk yourself into it, you will end up just as successful once you are a superman. It could be just as simple as allowing yourself to be the superman or it could be a long journey through yourself before you come to the realization that you have just as much ability as anyone else to be a superman along with us.

Chapter 4 - Spread Love and Compliments

Spread love. What we aim for as supermen is to spread love and the want for improvement. No, it's not always physical love or signs of affection. It's as simple as complimenting someone on something nice they did or some feature that you like about them. Complimenting something they are wearing is a compliment to a choice they made and it will make them feel good. Any time you can compliment somebody on something, do it. Make sure that people know you as the person who compliments people without expecting anything in return for it. Be the person people like to be around because he noticed their haircut or that they finished their paperwork for the week early. People don't expect to be complimented for things that are expected of them. This is one of the biggest areas that is overlooked by those of us who like to compliment others, make them feel good about themselves and spread love in general. **It's not fair to notice every time someone does something wrong but never that they are doing what is right.** Do everything you can to squash negativity and spread love. Love is the best feeling any of us can have and it is one of the least describable. Every single person you talk to will give you a different definition of love. The value of love is beyond that of money and can even go beyond the elation from self-improvement. It is one of the easiest things to give other people and there need not be a limit on the amount of it available to you and everybody else. You don't have to love the things they do or even how they act, you just have to love them for being alive and going through what all of us fight through every day.

Section X - Celebrate Any Time You Can

Do it responsibly of course. By celebrate I don't mean plan an elaborate event and spend a lot of money on a party just because you finished your paperwork this week. What I mean is take a moment to celebrate any success you reach. Even if it is finishing the paperwork this week. This will reinforce how good it is to be successful and accomplish things. Don't use this celebration as a distraction or an excuse to waste time, use it as encouragement and self-satisfaction that you are moving in the right direction.

A lot of people say you don't deserve to feel successful for things you are expected to do. This is not true. The superman appreciates every success in life even though the superman expects it as well. It feels good. It should feel good. Let it feel good and appreciate that it does.

Just the other day I was walking down the street and saw a woman holding a baby. She was looking thoughtful or maybe just thinking something that wasn't making her smile. When she looked in my direction I made full eye contact and held a genuine smile of love toward her. I saw the difference it made for her. She started to smile and I could see in her eyes that she was feeling a genuine sense of love and happiness that there was in the world. Seeing that I created that within her made all the difference for me. We both had a much better day because of it. This is a feeling that can't be bought. It is something the superman is thankful for. It resonates on a much deeper level than the lives we normally live. The superman goes out of the way to make sure to spread love in the world even if it is simply for the stranger that walks by on the sidewalk. People are not strangers to us, they are life and so are we. Supermen recognize the importance of other people in the world and how by changing one person, we change their whole world.

Supermen can go to other supermen and share their success to spread and share love. Seeing other supermen do well encourages us to do well, shows us how possible it is, and that it is happening every day. You are not just living your life, you are living the life of all of those around you and it needs to be as loving as possible in every area including the small successes we have every day. Everyone appreciates being noticed for something they do, especially if they didn't do it to be rewarded. People who do things for the reward rarely benefit as much from it and don't get as much out of it as people who do it to spread love. We do things to make the world a better and more successful place for all of us. That is more of a reward than anything else could ever be.

Who do you know in your life that would benefit from improving? Is it really possible that any of them wouldn't benefit? It isn't. Improvement is for everybody. People may think it's silly at first, but constantly reassure them they have the ability just as you do to improve life for everybody, especially the person most important to them (themselves).

Share this book with them, share the mentality, teach it to them like someone else did for you (even if it was just reading this book that convinced you to make your life better). Help them make their list of goals and brainstorm things that would make them feel better in day-to-day life. It is always possible. Just look at all of the people in prison today that take better care of themselves than you do! They spend their time working out, reading, and being social. When reentered into society these people have developed a life of self-improvement that some of us could only dream of and never reach after years of self-improvement courses. The biggest thing holding them back, beside themselves, is that nothing is encouraging them to strive for more. Contentment (stagnation) is the biggest factor in stopping people from striving for more. Sometimes you have to help people see what is in their life so that they can improve. It will be incredibly easy for these people to agree with what you are saying (they will) but it will be a struggle to get them to practice it. Again, talk is cheap. It is up to you to be there next to your fellow supermen improving yourself along with them.

This can be as simple as smiling more often or as complex as climbing Mount Everest. Make sure their goals are close enough to your own if you're going to go so far as to climb Mount Everest. Just because you want to motivate someone else doesn't mean you should live their life instead of your own. You need to have your own goals that are just as fulfilling to you as theirs are to them. Part of being one in this group is that you will have other people with the same goals. There is always someone out there that wants to do what you do and there is someone here that wants to do what your friend wants to do. Talk to others and we will announce that you or your friend is looking for people with this specific goal. Even if there is no one right now, there will be in the future. **The one thing we all have in common is the main goal of bettering ourselves and our lives as well as helping those around us to better themselves and their lives.**

So now is the time you must decide. It doesn't take a lot to be as good as everybody else. Anybody can do it. Being human is easy but it's not going to be very fulfilling. If you're going to do something, do your best at it and be the best you can. The same is true for life. If you're going to live, be your best at it and be successful. We are supermen because we decided being man was too easy and wasn't very much of an achievement. People have been human for a very long time and they will continue to up until the very end. The choice I am asking you to make right now is to do yourself a favor and be more than human. I want you to be the superman so you can rise above with us and make the world a better place for you, for me, for everyone. Will you agree to be a superman along with us for your own success and the greatness that we can create for mankind? Once the world ascribes to our point of view, to be superman, there will no longer be man. There will be only supermen. In the future to be man will mean something much greater because the only term they will know for man will be the supermen we have created. They will then go on to develop a further term for what they still have yet to become and it will be great, as now the superman is for us. It is not out of our reach. We all have the ability we just need the determination and to make a conscious decision right now to follow the path to freedom and success.

PLEDGE

I, __________ agree to live up to my full potential and to strive for no less than the greatest of success in everything that I do. I agree to schedule my time wisely and to shape my life for success by removing anything that stands in my way or holds me back. I agree to teach others what they have inside of them and the capability that they are overlooking to become one of the greatest beings in the world. I agree to be the superman to it's fullest extent; to better myself and all of those around me in every way possible. I agree to cultivate my creativity and to keep up the struggle in everything I put my mind to. I agree never to accept failure or defeat but to keep on trying until I have achieved full success. I want to be the best possible me and I am willing to take all of the necessary steps to get there. I am a superman. I am the superman. The superman will always be a part of me and I will always be a part of the supermen. Together I am part of something bigger. We will make the world better for all of those that live in it and for future generations. We will accept nothing less than the complete spread of our message. From this day forward I will live the super-mentality and preach the word of the superman to all of those in need. I will do everything I can to live the best life by constantly working toward success and greeting each day with determination. I am now and always will be the superman.

______________________ ______________________

Sign Print

____

Date

Congratulations! You have made the first step and made the commitment to constantly improve yourself and the world around you by spreading love and the desire for more. I have no doubt that you will be the most successful you can be if you read, reread and practice everything here and in the sources of knowledge mentioned in the further reading notations. You have made the first step toward being the superman. The superman has always been a part of you and a part of all of us. It is now that we will let him out and make leaps and bounds in the success of our group. You are ready now to go out and live. This is the first day of your life as a superman; do all that you can and make the schedule for a rounded life of improvement that will become part of a legend. The legend of the supermen. It is us. It is here. It is now.

FURTHER READING

The Bible: King James Version
Bowker, John - *World Religions*
Brooks, Jennifer - *Everyday Mindfulness - Change Your Life by Living in the Present (Mindfulness for Beginners)*
Burns, David D. M.D. - *Feeling Good: The New Mood Therapy*

Carnegie, Dale - *How to Stop Worrying and Start Living*
Carnegie, Dale - *How to Win Friends and Influence People*
Carter-Scott, Cherie - *Negaholics: How to Overcome Negativity and Turn Your Life Around*
Clason, George S. - *The Richest Man in Babylon*
Conwell, Russell H. and Wanamaker, John - *Acres of Diamonds*
Covey, Stephen - *7 Habits of Highly Effective People*

Dass, Bhagavan - *It's Here Now (Are You?)*
Dass, Ram - *Be Here Now*
Dean, Jeremy - *Making Habits, Breaking Habits*
De Botton, Alain - *Religion for Atheists: A Non-Believer's Guide to the Uses of Religion*
Dispenza, Joe - *Breaking the Habit of Being Yourself: How to Lose Your Mind and Create a New One*
DK Publishing - *The Religions Book*
Duncan, Shannon - *Present Moment Awareness: A Simple Step-by-Step Guide to Living in the Now*

Epictetus and Dobbin, Robert - *Discourses and Selected Writings*

Gladwell, Malcolm - *The Tipping Point: How Little Things Can Make a Difference*

Helmstetter, Shad - *What to say When you Talk to Yourself*
Hill, Napoleon - *Think and Grow Rich*
Hogan, Kevin - *The Psychology of Persuasion: How to Persuade Others to Your Way of Thinking*

Isaacson, Walter - *Steve Jobs*

Johnson, Spencer - *Who Moved my Cheese?*

Kahneman, Daniel - *Thinking, Fast and Slow*
Klauser, Henriette - *Write it Down, Make it Happen*

Lichten, Joanne V. - *Dining Lean*

Mackay, Harvey B., - *Swimming with the Sharks Without Being Eaten Alive: Outsell, Outmanage, Outmotivate, and Outnegotiate Your Competition*
Maxwell, John C. - *Failing Forward: Turning Mistakes into Stepping Stones for Success*
McGonigal Ph.D, Kelly - *The Willpower Instinct*
McWilliams, Peter - *You Can't Afford the Luxury of Negative Thought*
Molloy, John T. - *Dress for Success*

O'Connor, Richard - *Rewire*
Orloff, Judith - *Emotional Freedom: Liberate Yourself from Negative Emotions and Transform Your Life*
Osho - *My Way: The Way of the White Clouds*
Osho - *For Madmen Only: Price of Admission - Your Mind*

Peale, Dr. Norman Vincent - *The Power of Positive Thinking*
Peres, Daniel - *Details Men's Style Manual*

Rothman, Lauren - *Style Bible*

Sachs, Jessica Snyder - *Good Germs, Bad Germs*
Satchidananda, Sri Swami - *The Living Gita: The Complete Bhagavad Gita - A Commentary for Modern Readers*
Scott, S. J. - *70 Healthy Habits*
Shove, Elizabeth - *Comfort, Cleanliness and Convenience*

Taylor, Eldon - *Choices and Illusions: How Did I Get Where I am and How Do I Get Where I Want to Be?*
Taylor, Michael - *Mind Maps*
Tolle, Eckhart - *The Power of Now: A Guide to Spiritual Enlightenment*
Tracy, Brian - *Goals!*

Urban, Hal - *Positive Words, Powerful Results: Simple Words to Honor, Affirm, and Celebrate*

Warshaw, Hope S. - *Eat Out, Eat Right*
Willett, Walter and Skerrett, P. J. - *Eat, Drink, and Be Healthy*
Wood, Evelyn - *Seven-Day Speed Reading and Learning Program*

Yogananda, Paramahansa - *Autobiography of a Yogi*

Ziglar, Zig - *Better Than Good: Creating a Life You Can Wait to Live*
Ziglar, Zig - *See You at the Top*

www.ingramcontent.com/pod-product-compliance
Lightning Source LLC
Chambersburg PA
CBHW071542040426
42452CB00008B/1089

* 9 7 8 0 9 9 6 6 7 5 1 0 9 *